Sorry Spock, **EMOTIONS DRIVE BUSINESS**

SORRY SPOCK,
EMOTIONS DRIVE BUSINESS

Proving the Value of Creative Ideas with Science

ADAM W. MORGAN

NEW YORK

LONDON • NASHVILLE • MELBOURNE • VANCOUVER

Sorry Spock, Emotions Drive Business

Proving the Value of Creative Ideas with Science

Published in New York, New York, by Morgan James Publishing. Morgan James is a trademark of Morgan James, LLC. www.MorganJamesPublishing.com

ISBN 9781642790719 paperback
ISBN 9781642790726 eBook
Library of Congress Control Number: 2018942591

Cover Design by:
Magdiel Lopez

Interior Design by:
Christopher Kirk
www.GFSstudio.com

Morgan James is a proud partner of Habitat for Humanity Peninsula and Greater Williamsburg. Partners in building since 2006.

Get involved today! Visit
MorganJamesPublishing.com/giving-back

Dedicated to my mentor—Ron Stone.

TABLE OF CONTENTS

Act III—Putting it all into practice.

PREFACE

I believe in ideas. Ideas can change the world. And creative ideas can certainly do a better job of building a brand.

Yet many in the advertising and marketing industries disagree. They consider creative ideas as marketing fluff. When recessions rise or profits plummet, their instinct is to stop using creative ideas and go back to straightforward and "logical" communications to save the day. Just the facts, ma'am.

They believe that so-called rational thought will prevail. That people will buy their products and services if they simply know all the superior product features and benefits.

Unfortunately, this strategy is just plain wrong.

Many books and studies have focused on proving that advertising works. It's no longer a debate. We know it works. But even bad advertising can work to some degree.

I want to prove that creative ideas work *better*. That emotional ideas actually boost the bottom line more than just a straightforward message. And I won't rely on popular case studies or creative examples that can be subjective.

I plan to use modern studies on the brain and neuroscience to prove that creative ideas work better. I'm going to show through logical and rational arguments that emotional advertising isn't fluffy. I'll show research that describes how good ideas can boost success. I'll logically explain why emotional ideas are actually a sound business practice, not the babblings of peculiar artists and creative misfits. It's the right way to communicate with customers—the right way to build a business. More than that, it's the best bet to improving the bottom line.

If marketing were simply a rational exercise, we would have landed on the perfect template by now. But it's not a perfect science. It's also an art. Even in today's digital environment, artificial intelligence and analytics won't solve all our marketing challenges. They're powerful tools that guide our strategies, but at the end of the day, emotional ideas are still the most powerful way to reach a customer's heart.

This book is written for the skeptics of creative advertising. The CEOs, marketing managers, accountants, VPs of sales, and anyone else who thinks it's a waste of time. The proof has been out there, but not necessarily all in one place.

I'm not claiming any new studies or discoveries on neuroscience, behavioral economics, or psychology. I'm a marketer, not a scientist. So if you are a scientist or psychologist and you've already drafted a negative Amazon review blasting me for not offering new research, you've missed the point. This book is not for you. This is not for those with a deep interest in neuroscience. You certainly know more on the topic. My intent is to reframe it all for creative pursuits in marketing and business. So feel free to delete that review. Seriously.

Today, we have a wealth of data on how the human brain makes decisions. Most of it is explained in academic journals or scientific studies that are complex. This book is intended as an executive review of all that science, so that you can understand the big picture as it relates to creativity. Like *Cliffs Notes* for business decision makers.

What makes this book different from other books on neuromarketing is that I plan to use all this great information toward a unique lens on creative marketing. Most other books in this category focus on how to improve your sales or to understand how customers make decisions. This is different. It's all about showing how creative and emotional ideas are a better way to communicate as marketers.

There's a new golden age of creativity that's about to begin. And it's based on the fact that science has finally caught up with creativity. Creative ideas are no longer a black box. Design-led companies are proving that emotional triggers equal a healthy profit. And creativity doesn't have to be a threat to strategic thought. It's time to stop relying on old and inaccurate instincts and start creating better experiences for our customers.

My hope is that we can move away from the typical battlefield of logic versus creativity, so that both have an equal seat at the marketing table. This debate has raged on for decades and we now have the data to end it. We need to better understand creative ideas so that they don't make marketers nervous. Because creative ideas shouldn't be scary.

And once you're convinced that creative ideas work better, the latter part of this book will explore ways that you can put all this knowledge into action. I'll review the basic marketing pitch that many agencies and experts use when showing how their ideas break through the clutter and reach your audiences. And then I'll describe that same process through the lens of neuroscience, so you know what's going on in your customers' heads when they see a creative message.

I'll also discuss how to recognize good ideas and offer a few ways to use this new understanding to make better marketing decisions. I'll discuss the right ways to measure and judge creativity. I'll also share a few examples to improve internal branding practices and how to build up your personal marketing gut so you can create better marketing plans and optimize your marketing with a balanced approach. And finally, I'll explore how to think more intuitively, so you can tap into your whole brain and become a dynamic leader.

And if you already believe in creative ideas, hopefully I can provide enough background and ammo, so you can help those who don't understand the value of creativity. Like that tricky client or internal stakeholder. You can challenge their built-in cultural biases and offer a logical argument for the need to balance both emotional and rational ideas. You can help them understand the value of design, emotional marketing, and content that drives a holistic customer experience. Or just hand them a copy of this book. (I know, too soon.)

It's time to embrace both logic and creativity as equals. So that when you are faced with a choice of publishing an emotionally charged idea, you won't avoid it and go with something safe. Because you will know how a creative idea will give you a bigger return on your marketing dollar.

ACT I—

THE NEED FOR CREATIVE IDEAS

Chapter 1

THE PITCH MEETING

"Well? What do you think? Which idea do you like best?"

I pointed again at the three billboard concepts mounted on foam core. Three completely different ideas that were created for a self-directed investment company. All three billboards delivered the brand message with unique headlines that would catch the attention of a consumer driving the daily commute to work.

When presenting ideas, the classic rule of three is important. It gives the decision maker a small range of options, but not so many that they experience choice paralysis.

My client, Russell Fisher, sat back in his chair while tapping his finger against his cheek.

"They're all great. But which one is going to be the most effective? Which one is really going to pull for us?"

I expected a response like this. Most clients ask this question of their ad agency. Which one does the agency think will work best?

Over the past two weeks, our agency team had worked hard on these billboard options. They represented a big opportunity to expand our work with Russell's company. The billboards were a test. If they were successful, we would expand the campaign nationwide. If they failed, budgets would be cut.

I looked around the small conference room to see if anyone else was going to jump in and answer Russell. This meeting was critical. I hoped he would like all three and have a hard time picking his favorite. Instead he was avoiding the choice and putting the pressure back on us.

When Russell asked which of the three options would be best, I had a response ready to go. The two others from my agency looked back at me with shrugs. So, like any trained ad guy, I went for it.

"They're all great concepts," I said. "And any of them could drive the results you want. They're all on brand. They have plenty of impact. And they all have a memorable concept that will help with retention. But if I had to pick a favorite, I'd go with option three."

Russell nodded but still wasn't convinced. He continued to tap his cheek. It was driving me crazy. After a moment of silence, he responded.

"I trust you," he said. "I believe you think these creative concepts will help me get more accounts. But here's the truth. My boss doesn't believe in creative ideas. He thinks we just need to put our logo on the billboard with a straightforward phrase that tells people what we do. He believes in just giving people some basic information and they'll make the right choice and sign up. No cutesy stuff."

The dreaded phrase. No cutesy stuff. No fluffy marketing. No creativity. I knew his boss believed in a more direct approach. But I was hoping Russell would love our ideas so much, he'd become an advocate and sell something up the chain. No luck. This pitch was failing. My stomach tightened.

I spent the next twenty minutes explaining why a boring, logical headline wasn't going to cut through all the clutter. I used all the standard arguments that twenty years of advertising experience had taught me. I explained why creative ideas are better because they pull on a consumer's emotions and how brands create a likeable personality. I suggested that people would just ignore a straightforward billboard and that it would be a waste of his budget.

I think I defended the creative well and he listened to all my arguments. But his next comment turned the conversation in a direction that I wasn't prepared to handle.

"I believe you," he said. "I really do. But how can I go back to my boss and explain how we just need to trust the guy from our ad agency? He won't follow your gut feeling. What hard proof do you have that creative headlines work better than regular straightforward ones? And I'm talking scientific, logical proof? Not marketing opinion."

I was disarmed. What real proof did I have? I sat and thought about his question, my mind sprinting for a solution. I was losing my opportunity.

I had my opinion on what type of advertising works. Creative ideas that spoke to emotions always pull better. But in my experience, many clients were afraid of these kinds of campaigns. They trusted hard numbers and logic. Creative ideas feel risky. Direct and logical ideas are safe.

To me, a safe idea was ineffective. Wallpaper, not marketing. But my reasons were based on *my* experience, not hard science. They were born from the marketing world of impact, likeability, social stickiness, and other subjective advertising terms. These are soft terms that we use to describe the emotions and feelings we get when we see a brilliant creative idea.

That's why there's an endless debate over creativity—because it's so subjective. We judge ideas based on how we react personally to them. Even the trusted logic of focus groups, award show judges, and research polls is flawed. They're still judging creative based on personal experiences.

Without all the marketing terms and without relying on my personal experience, every rational reason I could say to Russell in that meeting would fall short. He wanted to know the answer to a very fundamental question in marketing.

In fact, his question that random day at an average client meeting in the spring of 2012 would make a big impact on my career.

What Russell was really asking is a basic question that our industry has been asking for years:

Do creative ideas work better?

He wanted to know if emotions are necessary in marketing. If all the storytelling and personality makes a difference. Or if we're wasting our time because people just want data. Just product benefits and logical reasons to buy.

And he wanted an answer that would satisfy someone who didn't believe in all the touchy feely, buzzwordy crap. No personal experience. No case studies of other creative brands. No award-show correlation. Just hard facts and science.

I'd grown up as a creative writer in the mid '90s, so at my core I believed that creativity was the solution. But all my arguments at this point were based on subjective experiences. I didn't have anything based on scientific, logical proof. For once, I was speechless.

The meeting ended a few minutes later. Russell thanked us for all the work and promised to let us know any feedback after showing it around the office and to his boss. But I knew what would happen.

I'm sure I mumbled something like, "I'll get back to you with a better answer," but as everyone left the conference room, I stayed behind. I sat there hoping I would discover one of those brilliant hindsight responses that you come up with when the heat of the moment is over.

Unfortunately, nothing came to mind.

Chapter 2

WHY WE NEED AN ANSWER

Weeks after the meeting, we shipped the final billboard art-work to the printers with a straightforward headline that simply explained what the company did. Nothing creative. Just the facts.

In the end, Russell's boss didn't see the value in trying a creative idea. He was worried that no one would get it. And he didn't want anything getting in the way of communicating basic information about the company. He referenced earlier work that pulled decent numbers and employed similar straightforward content.

In reality, the billboard was a failure. It didn't pull in many new accounts. A year later I noticed it was still up, with the vinyl starting to fade and crack—always a reminder to me that I didn't have an answer.

I couldn't stop thinking about Russell's question. In fact, it really cut deep into my core beliefs about creativity. During the '90s, I became a devout student of the creative revolution. I believed that creative ideas were always the better choice. I had surrounded myself with great creative work. I had slaved on countless projects to come up with creative concepts. I knew deep in my gut when an idea was good or bad.

But now, without the benefit of trusting my gut, I had to think really hard about how I could convince someone who didn't have my creative upbringing to believe in good ideas. Sure, a creative person at an ad agency understood the value of a creative idea. But most decision-makers had backgrounds in finance and data. They had a completely different point of view.

A dividing question since the '70s.

The question over the impact of creative ideas has been a struggle for decades. This story of art versus science and left brain versus right brain started in the '70s when creative advertising was born.

Two famous men helped bring these two schools of thought to the forefront of advertising.

The poster boy for analytical advertising strategy was David Ogilvy. His successful work built an advertising agency that still stands today. His famous book, *Ogilvy on Advertising*, explained his secrets to advertising success. He had this whole advertising thing down to a science. Literally.

In his book, he explains in great detail the exact process you should use to create an effective advertisement. How many words should be used in a headline. What type of image you should use. Where that image should be placed on the layout. He described the formula of thirds, where the top third of the page was your headline, the middle a picture, the bottom a paragraph of detailed information about your product.

Here's a taste of Ogilvy's perspective on advertising: "I do not regard advertising as entertainment or an art form, but as a medium of information. When I write an advertisement, I don't want you to tell me that you find it 'creative.' I want you to find it so interesting that you buy the product."[1]

It was all very logical. He sold his formula to dozens of the nation's biggest companies and made truckloads of money. He was at the top of his game.

Perhaps much of this sounds familiar. Today there are dozens of experts who are ready to explain to you the science and best practices behind good marketing. This includes the correct length for a tweet, the optimal number of images for a blog post, and the right moment in an online video to flash your call to action. The medium may change but the problem is still the same. Many still believe it's just a logical process.

Bill Bernbach didn't agree. He didn't follow Ogilvy's rules. In fact, he tried to break every one of them.

Bernbach believed there was a better way to be effective. He taught the creative minds in his agency to think outside the norm. They created ads that didn't use any formulas or scientific practices. They simply created emotional communications that resonated with the audience.

Many of his ideas are forever canonized in our industry as some of the most famous and effective ads in history. Ideas such as his "Think Small" campaign to launch the Volkswagen Beetle.

Bill never wrote a book about his marketing beliefs, so a few of the people who worked at his agency decided to do it for him.[2] The book described his creative philosophy and was loaded with interesting quotes and examples of his work. The book was intended more as a tribute to Bill, and for a while it was only printed in a limited quantity. Today, it's difficult to find.

Bernbach's approach gave birth to a new way of communicating. As people who worked with him moved to other ad agencies, a new creative culture emerged. He was called the father of creative advertising, and his approach started a creative revolution.

Here's how Bernbach explained his advertising philosophy, "However much we would like advertising to be a science—the fact is that it is not. It is a subtle, ever-changing art, defying formulization, flowering on freshness, and withering on imitation; where what was effective one day, for that very reason will not be effective the next, because it has lost the maximum impact of originality."[3]

As the creative advertising movement grew in strength, the scientific agencies adapted. They positioned themselves in order to stand out from all the creative agencies by becoming a "results" agency.

A results agency boasted a process that didn't rely on all the cutesy creative crap. They offered businesses a logical approach that was based on numbers and research. Armed with facts, they could solve your marketing problems in a way that produced concrete results. The new banner of *strategy* gave courage back to the accountants. They were being smart with their marketing money, while all those creative people were just pissing away pennies.

How both sides prove they're right.

Even today, most advertising agencies claim to be on one side or the other. You are either a "creative" agency or a "strategic" agency.

On the company side, it's a similar struggle. Some companies believe in branding, where you use creativity over the long term to build up a company. Other companies believe in direct marketing and lead generation, where it's all about the numbers and volume to grow.

It has been an endless battle of the left brains versus the right.

Both sides try to prove why their approach is superior with endless case studies and sales numbers. There are countless books (and advertising agency websites) that try to prove one viewpoint or another. One side points to the latest brand campaign as proof that creativity drives results. Later, the other side uses the same campaign as proof that a solid strategy and data insights are the reason for success.

So here's why we need an answer to Russell's simple question.

The problem is that every situation is so organic and separate from the other, that it's hard to know which approach is truly more effective. The real reasons get muddled and each side can spin the story to meet their argument.

This is why I haven't used any case studies in this book. They're too subjective.

What we need is a neutral answer to the debate. One that isn't subjective. Because we can all benefit from knowing how to navigate the benefits of both creativity and strategy.

A greater need for an answer today.

Now that we know the situation and the need for an answer. The next question is, why now? We've been debating creativity versus results for years, and businesses on both sides are thriving.

The reason is that with the rise of digital, the pressure of accountability is greater than it has ever been. Marketers and advertisers are all on the hook to deliver results. Every CMO and CEO and CFO wants to know if all the money they're spending on advertising and marketing is worth the expense.

In past decades, if the cash register rang, you were doing your job as an advertiser. Few questions were asked. Today your accountability is much more pronounced.

One of my previous bosses, Dave Sollitt, told a story of when he was a young account executive working for a large advertising agency in the early '80s. He worked on a major beer account and was charged with balancing the advertising budget against the actual spend. It was his first job and he wanted to impress the client.

Unfortunately, during the reconciliation process, he couldn't figure out where $200,000 had been spent. For a week before a big status meeting with the client, he scanned and double-checked every expense. He never found the missing cash.

The day of the status meeting, he knew he was going to be fired. With slumped shoulders, he presented the budget and explained to the room of executives that he couldn't account for $200,000 of their advertising spend.

The room was silent for a long minute as the executives looked side to side at each other with concerned brows. Then the room erupted in applause.

Dave was confused. He was expecting to be ripped to shreds in front of the group. Eventually one of the executives spoke up, "Well done, young man! I believe that's the least amount of money that's been unaccounted for in the past decade. Good job in getting us the closest we've ever been to a balanced budget."

Years later, Dave would still laugh at how imprecise advertising used to be. But no longer. Today with all the hypersensitivity to be more productive and find more ways to cut costs, the measurements of success have a much smaller margin of error.

There's an old quote by John Wanamaker where he said, "Half the money I spend on advertising is wasted. The trouble is, I don't know which half."

Today, we know so much more. We have more sophisticated tools that measure every click, hover, open, call, and close. And even though the majority of the data is coming from online media, we've created alternate ways to measure traditional media like billboards, print, and broadcast. We measure bumps in organic search and campaign lift based on overlaid media schedules. We do everything possible to prove that our marketing is successful.

In the era of digital marketing, we have to show very specific metrics that spell out consumer behavior long before they reach the end of the funnel. We have to stretch dollars with every project. We are able to see exactly who is responding to what messages on what device at an exact moment in time. It's an amazing time where we no longer have to guess at which half of our marketing efforts is working. We can create more personalized experiences than ever before. In fact, we're looking for so much detail in the data that we often promise predictions of future results.

The good news of our current era is that we have answers for the accountants because we have the metrics to validate our advertising budgets.

The bad news is that some executives no longer trust the guts of experienced marketers, but only rely on the numbers. The result is that creative ideas are being questioned more and more as some leaders don't feel that creative ideas are the reason for success.

Data is the future of marketing. And we are discovering more ways to use data to create better experiences. We all agree on that. Where this book is concerned is how we use that data. Just because we have more data, does that mean that creativity isn't necessary?

Data isn't the enemy of creativity. It helps us refine our messages. It provides guidance and best practices. Where we need help is in the conference room long before a website or ad goes live, where decision makers select which idea to use.

Digital is increasing the pressure. We're all more accountable. We all need to put our money and time into the most effective solution. We want to know the ROI on our marketing spend.

Without proof that creativity is more effective, the typical business reaction is to avoid it. That's why we need an answer today.

We need to know, now more than ever, if creative ideas work better.

Chapter 3

WHAT CREATIVITY BRINGS TO THE TABLE

I believe most marketers want to do the right thing. We want to succeed. We want to communicate the right way with our customers. Unfortunately, it's so much easier in a meeting to point out an objective reason why we shouldn't use a creative idea.

I've seen this happen hundreds of times. When faced with a choice of a creative idea versus straightforward information, some end up choosing the latter. Because it feels like the safe answer.

Let's face it, creative ideas can be scary.

Lee Clow, the chief creative officer of TBWA\Worldwide, once described this relationship of fear and creativity in a simple tweet.

"Most ideas are a bit scary, and if an idea isn't scary, it's not an idea at all."[4]

For many of us, creative ideas are the unknown. We may not understand how others come up with creative ideas and we've been taught in business to avoid risk.

Then a creative idea comes along and it makes us feel something. But in business school, we learned that business is a rational choice. Those who succeed are smart, not emotional. Emotions are something we have learned to push away. Emotions are beneath serious thinkers and rational leaders. Through logic and analysis, you will make good decisions and succeed in business.

But what if you understood emotions better. What if you opened the curtain and learned more about emotional ideas. If you took a rational approach to understanding creative ideas. Then it's no longer scary.

I know some creative people try to shroud the creative process in mystery. And make it seem like it's hard to come up with creative ideas. But it's not. You can approach creativity with a rational perspective. I do it all the time.

Throughout my twenty-three years in this industry, I have viewed creativity differently than most creative types. Creativity isn't a Zen thing where I magically stumble into ideas. I look for patterns and break apart the process, looking for balanced ways to solve creative problems.

By the end of this book, you should have a much better understanding of what a creative idea is all about. Which means you can retrain yourself to avoid reacting based on culture and start reacting with an open mind.

Let's start with a simple principle that is foundational to all the science we're about to review:

A creative idea is basically an emotional idea.

It can be that simple. Creative ideas tap into our emotions and make us feel something. This can be any emotion. It can be humor or sadness or fear or insight. Many leaders think that an emotional ad is just trying to be silly. Or too heartfelt.

Success is finding that perfect emotion to fit your brand—in that specific moment, where you can connect with a customer for the right reasons. That is what a creative idea should do. It's a fact or a data point, surrounded by something that taps into your emotions.

That something could be storytelling, or art, or a combination of visuals and words. But the final effect is the same. It makes you feel something.

Some worry that their customers will push away their feelings, too. And then the piece of communication won't work. More often, the emotional idea never sees the light of day. Even though we may laugh or feel something in the meeting where the ideas were presented, our instinct is to avoid emotions. So we go with the logical and safe idea instead.

But emotional ideas don't have to be a mystery. In this book, we'll discuss more detail about emotions, what makes them, and how you can use them to create better customer experiences that will improve your bottom line.

It's funny, the more we understand our emotions, the more we can approach them with a rational point of view.

Design thinking and empathy.

In a *Wired* article titled "The origins of design thinking," Jeffery Tjendra explains how the act of creativity has been turned into a logical process.

"When design thinking is applied to business by making creativity logical, the results are tremendous."[5]

Tjendra describes how companies that only manage innovation with logic and analytical thinking will be disrupted. But the companies that understand the value of creative thinking will thrive.

Sure, design thinking is a buzzword, but only because it has been proven to be successful. It's now the framework for modern business innovation and has been adopted by companies around the world.

Another creative approach that is disrupting business is the idea of a design-led company. A design-led business is one that prioritizes the design process in everything it does. All business decisions and structure are built around the belief that design and creativity are the only way to differentiate your company.

In Silicon Valley, this trend is the new gospel. New startups and old tech giants are preaching the values of design thinking and design-led management.

The beauty of this trend is that businesses are starting to once again accept creativity as a serious business practice. They recognize that creative problem solving is a necessary approach to improve the bottom line.

And the analysts agree. Creativity, design, and great experiences are the new competitive advantage. Established companies that don't embrace these emotional connections risk falling behind.[6]

The big issue, however, is how to integrate these principles into your business. Traditionally, the best type of employee to elevate design thinking in your company is a designer. Why? Because designers have been trained in the art of emotion.

One of the core principles of design thinking is empathy. And creative people have been immersed in the ideas and methods that create empathy. They have trained themselves to be extra sensitive to emotional ideas and concepts.

Creative people are drawn to emotion. They feel more when viewing art. They connect quickly with storytelling. And they're rabid consumers of media and pop culture. They love anything with a creative pulse.

As a creative veteran, I get it. For decades, I've surrounded myself with creative ads that span the spectrum of emotions. I've studied decades of funny TV spots, read hundreds of inspiring stories, and analyzed every heart-rending ad in the award shows.

And over the years, my sensitivity to emotion has grown. Almost too much. I cry at every animated movie I watch with my kids. And

I can no longer watch some drama films. (I cried for thirty minutes straight after watching *A Beautiful Mind*. Whew.)

It's this intense training and exposure to emotion that makes a good creative mind. That's why creative people can more easily discover a great creative idea. Or solve a problem in an unorthodox way. They can feel it. They've trained their brains to react to the slightest hint of emotion in any piece of communication.

To them, creativity isn't scary because they've trained themselves to feel it. This is why the best way to help your business move toward creative innovation is to hire a creatively trained brain. Give deign a seat at the executive table.

The other option is to teach yourself to be more sensitive to emotions. I know this goes against our modern education system, but one of the best ways to know if creative ideas work is to first be able to recognize them. It just may take some time for you to get there.

But even with all the success of design-led thinking, high-touch creative, and experience-led businesses, many are still making marketing decisions based on an old framework that logic is supreme. We still place all our trust and base our goals on numbers. No emotions.

Unless business decision makers understand today's new creative environment, we will continue to flounder. Unless we put creativity and logic on equal footing, we are missing out on marketing that can truly impact the bottom line.

This is the crossroads where we find ourselves today. And the purpose of this book. Should we try a creative idea or stick to a logical idea if we want better results? Do creative ideas really work better or not?

It's time to dive into the science behind creativity.

ACT II—

THE SCIENCE BEHIND CREATIVITY

Chapter 4
THE BRAIN INSIDE

One of the first companies that I helped create advertising for was Intel.[7] It was during the mid 1990s when the CPU was the poster child of the PC. Thanks to a brilliant tagline—The Computer Inside—Intel was able to convince consumers that the CPU was the most important part in a personal computer.

For the first time, they put the logo of a single component (one of hundreds) on the outside of the computer. The Intel microprocessor became the main differentiator in selecting the quality of a PC. The Intel Inside campaign was successful for a solid decade and helped Intel experience unprecedented growth.

Since then, the idea that the microprocessor rules the computer has continued to be a part of our digital culture. But as more people become computer nerds and are expert at understanding all the necessary components of a computer, the dominance of the microprocessor begins to fade.

Certainly, consumers still care about the processor. But with a greater collective knowledge of computers and their components, other factors become just as important—like the size of the hard drive, the quality of the video card, and the type of screen.

In the same way, many believe that the CPU of our brains—our executive function or our rational thought—is more valued than our other mental capacities.

But as we begin to better understand how the brain works, how all the various parts connect and function, and how this affects our choices and actions, the dominance of logic also begins to fade.

Yes, logic is important, but it's not the only thing that matters. And while most of us have no intention of becoming neuroscientists, a basic understanding of the various parts of the brain and how they function is extremely helpful.

Years ago, psychologists could only guess at what was happening in our minds. But with advances like fMRI machines that scan our brains in real time and provide images that map our neural activity, we now know more. No, we don't know everything. But collectively, we have amassed thousands of research studies that offer more accurate answers.

In the past few decades, scientists have made astounding discoveries about how our brains actually work. Thanks to years of research with modern technology and behavioral studies, they've been able to explain exactly what happens in our brains when we react to messages, when we analyze choices, and when we make a decision. We now have a small window into seeing what we are thinking in specific situations. That said, this knowledge is only useful when we provide context and apply it to our individual careers.

So let's start this journey off by clearing up a few myths about the brain and better understanding the science behind creative marketing.

The forest from the trees.

I often introduce myself as a central brainer. No, I'm not claiming to have a third section wedged between the two hemispheres. Let me explain.

Having built a career in a creative industry, I've seen firsthand the extremes of traditional left- and right-brain thinking.

I've worked with dozens of graphic designers, art directors, photographers, and writers. Many of them are the classic example of an artistic or creative thinker. They are ultra-talented when it comes to visual arts and abstract ideas. But to others, they have their heads in the clouds and they create in a very organic way. They can't explain how they come up with ideas or craft beautiful art. They just "feel" it. And if you start talking numbers, statistics, or logic, their eyes glaze over and they lose all interest.

I've also worked with just as many project managers, financial accountants, operations managers, and compliance officers—traditional left-brain thinkers. They live in spreadsheets and Gantt charts. They're talented at understanding process and attention to detail. They feel comfortable with a linear flow. They love a solid strategy they can execute. And when it comes to creating new ideas, they feel out of their comfort zone and often prefer to leave all that to the creative department.

As for my career, I've worked on both sides. First as a copywriter and creative director, creating campaigns based on big ideas and original concepts. Later as a strategist and marketing manager, supervising budgets, timelines, and approvals.

I learned to build my creative muscles and also to understand how business works. As I felt comfortable wearing both right- and left-brained shoes, I considered myself somewhere in the middle— able to create and sell.

At first, I thought that describing myself as a central brainer would resonate with others. They wouldn't quickly judge me as belonging to one camp or the other. Both sides would accept me. I figured wrong.

To be honest, it mostly just confused people and required a longer explanation. But once I muddled through my abstract description, I discovered that there are many others in this world who would describe themselves in a similar way. I had found my tribe. People who are comfortable in both the business and creative worlds.

Of course, with basic research on the topic, it's clear that there really isn't anything factual about the idea of being a central brainer. It's not an anomaly. Because the truth is, I use both sides of my brain equally. Just like every other person on earth. We all use the whole noodle. So I guess I'm just a regular old whole brainer.

Just like my misconception of being a central brainer, some of our traditional ideas about the brain aren't completely accurate. Like how emotions cloud your judgement. Or why we all react like cavemen because of our croc brains. A few of these myths are perpetuated in presentations and conference sessions on neuroscience. What's more interesting, however, are the insights that most of us don't know about.

To clear things up, we'll start by describing a few of the basic parts of the human brain and how they relate back to creative advertising. And while I'm not going to describe each specific chunk of the brain, as this isn't a primer on neuroscience, it's important to understand them in general terms.

The computer in your head.

Let's dig deeper into the earlier metaphor with Intel where we compare our brains to the working parts of a simple computer. It's a metaphor that's certainly overused, but it works.

Imagine for a moment that your brain is like a computer. It's made of three basic parts: a massive hard drive, the latest CPU processor, and several input devices.

Here's how it works. The input devices (i.e., your eyes, ears, nose, and skin) all send millions of pieces of data into your computer. These represent your life's experiences and what you observe in your environment.

The CPU is your executive function. Your executive function handles all the logic. It processes new experiences and then sends them to your hard drive. Technically, your executive function also includes your RAM and short-term memory. For this metaphor, we'll refer to all of this logical stuff as your conscious thought or your CPU.

Your hard drive is the bulk of your brain. It holds all your memories and acts as your long-term storage. Most of what happens on your hard drive is in your subconscious. We can't consciously remember every memory that's stored on your hard drive, deep in the folds of your brain. Sure, we can recall some, but most are locked away unless something triggers the memory.

The bulk of the first half of this book will focus on the CPU and hard drive and how they interact because most of the interesting action happens between your CPU and your long-term memory. Our CPU represents our logical thoughts and our hard drive holds our emotions.

Of course, in reality, the brain is much more complex. This simple metaphor breaks on many levels for hardcore scientists. I only introduce it as it helps explain complexity in more simple terms throughout the book.

Right versus left.

In marketing, discussions about logical strategy versus creative ideas usually come back to the idea of our brain being split into two halves. The left is known for logic, the right is known for creativity. You're either a creative type who uses more of your right hemisphere. Or you're a logical strategist who favors the left hemisphere.

But the two halves of our brains actually do so much more.

The left hemisphere is the master of *denotation*. It helps you understand the literal meaning of things. The facts. Like a dictionary, it helps with definitions of the elements in our world. When you see the written word *hat*, it interprets that word into the literal meaning—an object placed on your head. The left prefers a linear chain of elements and provides structure and rules. It helps us see each individual tree.

The right hemisphere helps us discover the connections between completely unrelated things. It provides the *connotation*. When you laugh at a joke, or you read a poem, or you understand a metaphor in a story—your right hemisphere helps you make the necessary connections so that you "get" the idea. It makes the linguistic connections. It brings the facts together and creates a story. Which means that your right brain helps you see the big picture. It helps you see the whole forest.

In other words, the left helps you understand the individual parts and the right makes sense of the sum.

Of course, with all the complexity in the world, just using one hemisphere or the other won't cut it. We can't consciously turn off one half and only use the other. Even those who lean more right or left aren't lopsided under their skulls. For example, artists don't have a really large right brain and a withering left. The reality is they have and use both sides.

We need both in order to understand the multifaceted environment that surrounds us. Ignore the old myth that we only use 10 percent of our brains. We use every little bit of our gray matter. We may just be unskilled at creating or retrieving certain memories, but that doesn't mean we aren't using everything.

So where did we come up with the idea that our left and right halves behave so differently? A good place to find the answer is by understanding the split-brain theory.

Crossing the streams.

The concept of the split-brain theory was pioneered by Roger Sperry.[8] In the 1950s and 1960s, Sperry and his colleagues worked with "split-brain" patients who had their corpus callosum severed to reduce violent epileptic seizures. The corpus callosum is the flat bundle of neural fibers that connects the two halves of our brains and allows them to share information back and forth.

With the corpus callosum cut, these patients in essence had two brains that worked independently. Sperry worked with several seizure patients and for the first time in history, we learned about each hemisphere's role. For example, he learned that our right hemisphere controls the left side of our bodies, and the left controls our right side. Or that language is mostly controlled by our left hemisphere.[9]

Even more interesting, he learned that each hemisphere has its own perceptions and impulses to act. With a few split-brain patients, they were literally of two minds. Usually the dominant side wins and the other side relents. But sometimes there can be a real conflict. For example, when one man would get dressed, sometimes he would pull his pants up with one hand, and the other hand would try to pull the pants back down. Once his left hand grabbed his wife to shake her in anger and his right hand defended her by grabbing the aggressive left hand.[10]

Beyond what we learned from Sperry and his patients, there are other real-world stories that give us insight into the relationship between the left and right hemispheres. Stories where people have either split brains or they are missing one half.

One interesting story is that of megasavant Laurence Kim Peek,[11] who was born without a corpus callosum. He had a rare birth defect where the corpus callosum never formed. So in essence, he had two independent brains his whole life.

Although he had developmental disabilities and couldn't button his shirt, he had an exceptional memory and was the inspiration for the character Raymond Babbit in the movie *Rain Man*.

In his life, Peek memorized and could accurately recall the contents of more than twelve thousand books. His two hemispheres adapted to the birth defect, and both sides were able to control language. Each side could read independent of the other. When he read a book, his left eye would scan the left page and his right eye would read the right page. This happened simultaneously, and each side retained half the story. Then Peek would piece together the two halves and remember the entire story. He spent a large part of his life in libraries and at home reading and memorizing books.

Another example of how our brains can adapt is the story of Cameron Mott.[12] She too suffered from extreme seizures and Rasmussen's syndrome, a condition where her own body attacked her brain cells. At age five, doctors removed half of her brain in order to stop her from having six to ten seizures a day. Miraculously, her remaining half was able to relearn important functions, and today she can walk and talk again. In essence, her left side was able to learn and perform functions usually limited to her right hemisphere.

There are even businesses that claim to help children and adults build new connections between neurons in order to improve learning and overcome mental issues. One example is the company Learning Techniques, which has had great success with their patented Physio-Neuro training.[13]

All these examples help demonstrate that our brains are remarkable at adjusting and learning new ways to survive. Our brains are dynamic and can rebuild new connections or relearn functions that have been disabled.

It also shows that it's difficult to make broad statements about which part of our brain does what. For example, earlier I said that language is usually controlled by the left hemisphere. But is that something we can say concretely? Cameron Mott proved that the right hemisphere can also control language.

How about the idea that only our left hemisphere controls all our logic and rational decisions? That's certainly a myth that has been perpetuated in popular culture. But is that really the truth?

Meet your frontal lobe.

Moving beyond traditional perceptions of the two hemispheres, the whole-brain story is more complex. We often talk of left versus right, but in reality, the story is more a drama between the front and the back.

There are several major parts of the brain that aren't often mentioned in casual conversations. One major part is the frontal lobe— the large area that spans both sides of the brain and sits at the front of your skull, just behind your forehead. A section of the frontal lobe, the prefrontal cortex, is a hallmark of more advanced homo sapiens compared to earlier primates and is linked to our executive function of thought (i.e., the CPU).

Our executive function covers a variety of actions, including our ability to determine good and bad, to balance better and best, and to work toward a defined internal goal. For example, it helps us put off immediate gratification for better future results.

This region of the brain has also been linked to a variety of important cognitive functions such as expression of personality, decision making, problem solving, good judgment, and understanding social behaviors. It's also linked to concrete rule learning. In short, the frontal lobe is unique to humans and is often the emphasis of studies that focus on human rationality.

This logical portion of the brain allows us to actually think about thinking. Our executive function lets us remove ourselves from our own point of view and have a front-row view of more than just what our senses are interpreting, but of what is actually being processed in our brains. This ability to think about what we are thinking is what allows us to compare better options, put off the now for the future, and care about more than just our self.

We'll talk more about the prefrontal cortex in later chapters. For now, it's simply important to know that our brain is complex. Logic isn't just found in the left hemisphere. It's a big part of the frontal lobe.

But we never have discussions about the front and the back half of the brain in terms of our logical brain and our emotional brain. Even though that makes as much sense for an argument similar to the left and right story.

No wonder many scientists prefer to talk about the *systems* of logic and emotion in our brains, rather than regions of the mind, as they are exceptionally balanced machines with billions of neurons that interconnect throughout the entire brain.

There's even debate on how many neurons the human brain contains. For years the oft-cited number was around one hundred billion. Then Dr. Suzana Herculano-Houzel decided to find out where that number originated. Nobody really knew. So she devised a way to measure it. She turned several brains that were donated to research into "brain soup" (as she put it) rather than the traditional method of chopping a brain into small pieces.

After counting the number of cell nuclei belonging to neurons, she placed the average number at around eighty-six billion neurons.[14] Which is still a massive amount. It's so many neurons, that she next tried to figure out how we, as humans, can create enough energy to keep our brains running.

Her secret to that question? Cooked food. "We can afford such a huge number of neurons. That difference might actually be related to a shift to a cooked food diet and that allows us to have far more calories per day. And with that we can afford a much larger number of neurons that other animals probably could not."[15]

The croc has croaked.

The left brain–right brain theory isn't the only idea about the brain that's leaked into popular culture. Over the past decade, even as recent as this year, I've heard several speakers at conventions explain the latest science on the brain in terms of the "triune theory."[16] This is commonly known as the theory of the croc brain or reptile brain.

Today, it's no longer embraced by the majority of neuroscientists. The basic theory is that the brain is made of three parts—the new brain (neocortex), the middle brain (limbic system), and the reptilian complex.

This idea, formulated in the 1960s by Paul MacLean, explains that the reptilian brain is our ancient brain that is connected to our basic fight or flight reflexes, similar to the forebrains of reptiles. The other two parts are more modern, culminating in our neocortex as the newest evolution that allows us to overcome and master our croc brain.

Starting around the year 2000, several discoveries debunked this theory. For example, the basal ganglia take up a smaller portion of reptile brains and birds—and most likely dates back to the common evolutionary ancestor of vertebrates rather than the origin of reptiles. Also, the neocortex was already present in the earliest emerging mammals.[17] This theory was referenced in many books from the 1980s and 1990s before it fell out of favor.

Embracing the whole brain.

The point in discussing myths or misconceptions isn't to analyze every theory or individual section of the brain. It's simply to highlight that the brain is complex. It's a massive amount of neurons that are constantly changing and adapting to our environment. Our brains are organic and vast.

The brain is still uncharted territory, even though we are learning more and more each day. With fMRI machines, we measure blood flow to certain areas when specific tasks are performed, but we can only infer so much. We know areas are active, but we can't see exactly what the brain is thinking.

So rather than focus on specific parts such as the left, the right, the front, or the inner reptile, we will focus on the distinct functions of the brain, regardless of where those functions live. Over the next few chapters, we will discuss the general systems that regulate both logic and emotion. This will help us grasp the relationship between the two and how that relates to marketing decisions.

The takeaway is that we require both logic and emotion to survive, because we use the whole brain—all the time. One side or function isn't more important than the other. To succeed, we need our left and our right brains. Connotation and denotation. CPU and hard drive.

We need to simultaneously see the forest and the trees.

Chapter 5

LOGIC ALONE ISN'T ENOUGH

On September 13, 1848, a near-fatal accident in Cavendish, Vermont, forever changed the world of neuroscience. It has become one of the most famous cases in brain research, both proving and disproving a wide variety of studies and theories.[18]

Twenty-five-year-old Phineas Gage was working for the railroad, helping blast away a section of rock for a new line of track. The process of blasting required drilling a hole, dumping in blasting powder, a fuse, and sand. Then the men would take a long metal rod to tamp the materials in the hole, so the explosion would break apart the rock, rather than just blast out the hole.

Unfortunately, as Phineas began the process of compacting, his tamping rod hit the side of the rock and created a spark. That spark lit the blasting powder, shooting the three-foot-seven-inch tamping iron into the air. The rod rocketed up through the base of Gage's jaw, behind his left eye, through his brain, and exploded out through the top of his skull. The sharp tip of the iron acted like a needle, creating a wide-open hole in his head.

Miraculously, Phineas lived. In fact, he was conscious and alert as the local doctor arrived to help bandage him up later that day. Unfortunately, a chunk of his frontal lobe was destroyed in the accident. According to the doctor, Phineas retained all his general intelligence and memory. And he eventually recovered, but his personality was never the same.[19]

Before the accident, Phineas was a hard-working, upstanding supervisor. After the accident, he indulged in the grossest profanity and became obstinate, with little regard for his fellows. He was impulsive, abandoning plans as quickly as they were devised. As doctors and scientists have studied his case over the years, there's been controversy over many aspects of Gage's recovery, mostly because of the lack of details.

However, in 1994, we finally discovered a link to Gage's change in personality. Neuroscientist Antonio Damasio published his book, *Descartes' Error*, which connected Gage's accident to other patients who, because of tumors or other accidents, had lost or damaged the same portion of the brain as Gage.[20] Damasio studied these patients in great detail, learning all he could about the effects of this missing portion of the brain.

The most famous of Damasio's patients was a man named Elliot. After a portion of Elliot's brain was removed because of a tumor, Elliot recovered and seemed to be a functional, intelligent person, just like Gage. Unfortunately, the removed portion of his brain was responsible for regulating his emotions.

Damasio performed a number of tests with Elliot to confirm that he was indeed incapable of emotion. For example, he attached a machine that tested Elliot's sweat glands as Damasio showed a variety of shocking images that always cause immediate emotional responses in normal patients, causing their hands to sweat.

No matter how disturbing the image, Elliot was never affected. He'd lost the ability to feel.

In all the hours of tests and studies, Damasio described him as never showing any sign of emotion. No sadness, no impatience, no frustration. Even when his life unraveled—he lost his job, his income, and even his wife left him—Elliot was completely dispassionate.

Elliot maintained a high IQ, but when forced to make a decision, he would deliberate for long periods of time on all the logical pros and cons of the decision. Simple choices such as where to eat would cause Elliot to debate the benefits and shortcomings of restaurants, distances traveled, and other factors that would influence the decision.

Through a variety of tests on Elliot and other patients, Damasio concluded that this inability to make decisions, even a simple decision, was the result of the missing part of their brains that processed emotions. The patient would be overwhelmed with logical thought, without the help of emotions to lock in decisions.

They would process and process endlessly. They would weigh the facts, but never arrive at a decision. And even if they made a decision, they would never feel good about it. They would go back and continue to analyze. They couldn't lock in a decision and move on—they kept evaluating. It's no surprise that Elliot's wife left him. She was going crazy with his constant processing of choices. It was all logic without any action. He had no connection to all his past good and bad decisions. He was starting from ground zero on every choice.

Should we put more value on logic or emotion?

Damasio describes how emotion and logic are not separate, but completely integrated. As noted in the title of his book, he shows how Descartes got it wrong. Descartes suggested that reason and emotion are opposing forces. Descartes writes about a homunculus, or a small man, inside our brain that helps us use logic to control the raging emotions or animal instinct inside us.

But in reality, the opposite is true. Humans rely heavily on both logic and emotions and use many parts of the brain throughout the entire decision-making process.

You can't silence emotion from a decision and rely solely on logic. Elliot and others proved that logic helps us understand decisions as we rationally weigh the good and bad. But you also need emotions to help your brain connect decisions with past experiences. Otherwise, you start from scratch on every single decision, just like many of Damasio's patents.

The insight from Damasio is that a brain that can't feel, can't make a decision. In other words, logic alone won't cut it. You can't drive the emotions from a human experience. To make a decision, you need to be able to feel.

This is the opposite of what many philosophers and intellectuals over the centuries have taught. Like Descartes, they taught that our rational or logical thought is supreme. And it needs to overpower our emotions in order for us to be a better human.

Take the famous statement from Descartes: "I think, therefore I am."[21] Descartes goes on to explain in his script *Habius Corpus* that rational thought and emotions are separate. Rational thought, Descartes argues, is the higher level, and emotions are a lower level of humanity. Rational thought is supreme, and emotions cloud your judgment.

He felt that our emotions are base and should be tempered, allowing our true intellect to shine. But what Damasio discovered is something that creative advertising has been telling us for years. That emotion is critical to making a brand decision. And not just at the first exposure, but throughout the entire decision-making process.

Unfortunately, when it comes to believing that rational thought is supreme, Descartes is not alone. The idea that logic is king is saturated into western culture.

Take medicine, business, and education. The only way to find truth or success is by following a logical pattern of steps that lead to a rational conclusion. Deep down in many of us, we feel that the best way to avoid bad decisions and succeed in life is to stop and think objectively about everything.

There is less trust in emotion. In fact, we often think emotions and instincts render the process invalid. Only rational thought from the logical areas of our brain, like the prefrontal cortex, is acceptable.

I often ask people what they really trust more, logic or emotion. If you honestly look deep inside yourself, it's a tough question to answer. From the scientific method to data measurement, our culture has trained us to believe that hard facts and logic always win. Emotions are a bit of a black box.

We'll come back to this question. But as we continue to explore the relationship between logic and emotion, really think about how you think. Don't just accept how culture or ancient philosophers would answer that question.

Are emotions animal instincts?

Descartes and Damasio aren't alone in asking the question of what makes us human. And the perception that our emotions are like animal instincts is a concern that many have considered.

Fortunately, two curious researchers from Harvard decided to figure out the true answer.

Cognitive psychologist Leda Cosmides and anthropologist John Tooby pioneered the new field of evolutionary psychology in the 1990s. Their goal was to understand the design of the human mind through a variety of disciplines including cognitive science, human evolution, neuroscience, and psychology.

In a famous study called *Evolutionary Psychology: A Primer*, they tackled the question of how our instincts guide us and the relationship between reason and instinct.

In the introduction to their study, they argue, "It was (and is) common to think that other animals are ruled by "instinct" whereas humans lost their instincts and are ruled by "reason", and that this is why we are so much more flexibly intelligent than other animals."[22]

These are pivotal questions. Said another way, are we human because we are rational and we can overpower our instincts? Do our emotions put us on the same level as animals, relying on instinct to guide our actions?

Through deep analysis, they discovered that we aren't more intelligent because we are more rational or logical. Just the opposite. It's because we have so many emotions or instincts that we're more intelligent beings.

"Human behavior is more flexibly intelligent than that of other animals because we have *more* instincts than they do, not fewer. We tend to be blind to the existence of these instincts, however, precisely because they work so well—because they process information so effortlessly and automatically.

"But our natural competences—our abilities to see, to speak, to find someone beautiful, to reciprocate a favor, to fear disease, to fall in love, to initiate an attack, to experience moral outrage, to navigate a landscape, and myriad others—are possible only because there is a vast and heterogenous array of complex computational machinery supporting and regulating these activities. This machinery works so well that we don't even realize that it exists—We all suffer from instinct blindness."[23]

When you think about the differences between humans and animals, our instincts are quite unique. Our fear of disease helps us live longer and keep our loved ones healthy. And the fact that we love others and care about strangers is yet another instinct that makes us a superior species.

What Cosmides and Tooby teach us in evolutionary psychology is that our emotions don't make us weaker. Our emotions are maybe our most valuable asset.

Learning to be creative.

Even with new insights from science that help us understand the relationship between logic and emotion, we're still molded by history and culture. Like Descartes' homunculus. Culture, both ancient and modern, has perpetuated the idea that logic is king.

A major example in our modern culture that's based on the model of supreme logical thought is our educational system.

In school, we're taught to only accept a rational thought as the correct answer. Our children are measured on the strength of their left and front brains. From how we measure success with grades to the methods we use for taking tests, it's all about facts and data.

Sure, we have elective classes such as art and sports, but even those classes are judged by the number of assignments produced and other data points. We don't measure success on how well children see the big picture or how they are skilled at connotation.

Several books have been written on our lopsided educational system, including Ken Robinson's book, *Out of Our Minds: Learning to Be Creative*,[24] where he describes a paradox in today's business environment. Companies are trying to compete in a world where technology is changing faster than ever. A world that needs innovative and creative thought and ideas. And yet most adults don't consider themselves highly creative.

Many children start out with a lot of creative instinct. But in our school systems, their creative talents are suppressed. Robinson argues that today's business problems could be solved if we could fix our school systems and retrain ourselves to think and value creative intelligence.

"Companies and organizations are trying to fix a downstream problem that originates in schools and universities. It would be naïve to think that education is simply a process of developing our natural abilities and rewarding achievements: that schools, colleges and universities simply sort out the intellectual sheep from the goats; that intelligent students do well and the less intelligent don't.

"Education doesn't just follow the natural grain of young people's abilities; it sorts them through two different filters. The first is economic: education categorizes people on implicit assumptions about the labour market. The second filter is intellectual: education sorts people according to a particular view of intelligence. The problem we face now is that the economic assumptions are no longer true and the intellectual filter screens out some of the most important intellectual abilities that children possess. There are drastic consequences for the development of creative abilities. This was always a problem, but now it's getting critical."[25]

He argues that this crisis is only getting worse. And the answer isn't to educate more people. We don't have a problem of not having enough graduates—we have too many graduates that have flooded the market. And most of these graduates have been educated in the same logical way. Some don't work well in teams, have a hard time communicating, and most of all, many can't think creatively.

"A major reason for this vast waste of ability in education is academicism: the preoccupation with developing certain sorts of academic ability to the exclusion of others, and its confusion with general intelligence. This preoccupation has led to an incalculable waste of human talent and resources. This is a price we can no longer afford."

His answer is to change the educational system. To have it value the benefits of creative thought and balance that with academic standards. We can't just raise our educational standards—we need to completely change them.

"To move forward we need a fresh understanding of intelligence, of human capacity and of the nature of creativity. Human intelligence is richer and more dynamic than we have been led to believe by formal academic education."

Robinson understands the need for both analytical and emotional intelligence. We need both to progress. "Conventional education separates intelligence from feeling, and concentrates only on particular aspects of the first. This is why being highly educated is no guarantee of emotional intelligence. Yet there is an intimate relationship between knowing and feeling: how we feel is directly related to what we know and think. Creativity is not a purely intellectual process. It is enriched by other capacities and in particular by feelings, intuition and by a playful imagination."[26]

Should right-brainers rule?

Our educational system isn't the only example of how the forces of logic and emotion are out of balance in our culture. Logic has dominated business for years, and author Daniel Pink points out the need for more emotional ideas in *A Whole New Mind: Why Right Brainers Will Rule the Future*.

Pink talks about how left-brain thinking has been a major part of our economy and has driven much of the growth in the past economic era. Knowledge-worker jobs like lawyers, accountants, and engineers ruled the information age.[27]

But times are changing, as the economy shifts toward a new age. And Pink explains how in the future, creative and emotional ideas will become the major force in driving key jobs and the economy. In the future, the jobs that companies will depend on will include inventors, designers, storytellers, big-picture thinkers, and meaning makers.

Pink refers to right brain, or creative thinking, as R-Directed thinking, and left brain, or logical and rational thought, as L-Directed thinking. (As I pointed out in the last chapter, there is more to the equation than just the two hemispheres, and the relationship of logic and emotion includes the front and back of the brain. For simplicity in this section, I'll refer to Pink's terms of left and right, so as to not confuse his arguments.)

Pink argues that for too long, rational thinking has been considered the less important half. And it's time we gave creativity an equal seat at the table.

He brings up three major reasons that are pushing the world toward a future that belongs to creative thinking, "Three forces are tilting the scales in favor of R-Directed thinking. Abundance has satisfied, and even over satisfied, the material needs of millions—boosting the significance of beauty and emotion and accelerating individuals' search for meaning. Asia is now performing large amounts of routine, white-collar, L-Directed work at significantly lower costs, thereby forcing knowledge workers in the advanced world to master abilities that can't be shipped overseas. And automation has begun to affect this generation's white-collar workers in much the same way it did last generation's blue-collar workers, requiring L-Directed professionals to develop aptitudes that computers can't do better, faster, or cheaper."

Thanks to today's abundance, everything we could ever want is readily available and extremely affordable. Which means we now look to designer labels on everything, including mundane products like a spatula. Pink details how design and the customer experience are the only way for companies to differentiate.

"In an age of abundance, appealing only to rational, logical, and functional needs is woefully insufficient. Engineers must figure out how to get things to work. But if those things are not also pleasing to the eye or compelling to the soul, few will buy them. There are now too many options. Mastery of design, empathy, play, and other seemingly 'soft' aptitudes is now the main way for individuals and firms to stand out in a crowded marketplace."

Which means companies need to use all the creative arts such as compelling design and storytelling to make amazing customer experiences. Or they face becoming irrelevant.

Many leaders and company executives are realizing how critical these types of experiences are to the bottom line. It's no longer enough to have a team of number-crunching MBAs. You need people who think about the customer journey, who make meaningful connections, and who create emotional moments with brands that are deeply personal.

Pink refers to these types of experiences as high touch and high concept. "Businesses are realizing that the only way to differentiate their goods and services in today's overstocked marketplace is to make their offerings physically beautiful and emotionally compelling. Thus the high-concept abilities of an artist are often more valuable than the easily replicated L-Directed skills of an entry-level business graduate."[28]

In this new conceptual age, creation and empathy are the new masters. In order to succeed, businesses need to create high-concept and high-touch experiences for their customers. The bottom-line results of today demand emotional and personal experiences. Straightforward facts and unemotional marketing are just like the knowledge worker jobs of the past era—outdated. If you want marketing and advertising that works, you need to champion emotional and creative ideas.

The argument that emotional skills are more important than logic in today's business environment is interesting. But just like being human, both are necessary. Which leads me to the question, does one have to overpower the other? Certainly in our business environment, the power has long sat with logic. But if we believe that the future will require more emotional skills, the answer should be giving emotion and creativity an equal seat at the table.

The experience is the difference.

While Daniel Pink describes a new era of creative jobs, executives at my own company, Adobe, are championing a similar idea. For Adobe, a company that balances both a history in the creative arts as well as deep data insights, this new era is all about creating deeply emotional customer experiences.

According to Shantanu Narayen, CEO of Adobe, the importance of the customer experience in today's digital business is paramount.

"Companies everywhere are doing great digital marketing campaigns. But if that's all we talked about, we'd be missing the point. Because digital experiences today have the power to transform every aspect of our life. They change the way we think, the way we travel, spend our money, do our jobs, and even relate to the entire world around us.

"We know today that some experiences are designed to blow our minds, and some have to go completely unnoticed and blend into our daily existence. No matter what the intent is, digital experiences need to be provocative, they need to be personal, and they need to be predictive. And they must work flawlessly and beautifully. This is the experience era."[29]

This is coming from a company that is leading the industry on data-driven marketing and analytics, as well as creativity tools, which is a great testament to the fact that in today's digital marketing world, data and creativity can live hand in hand.

Many companies who are trying to transform in order to compete in the digital age are only focused on the data. They spend lots of money on systems that process big data, but ignore the emotional side. They don't create experiences that connect with people, just data that connects with systems.

Logic and data alone will never rule the marketing world. Data isn't the end, but the beginning. Data inspires creativity. And creativity requires a foundation of rational thought. The future isn't about one or the other. It's the perfect balance of both logic and creativity.

This idea of creating personal and emotional experiences is something that many enterprise businesses understand and believe in. Some CEOs today look very different than their equals a few decades ago. Today, they must embrace more creative and soft tactics such as storytelling and design in order to grow business.

This new breed of business, namely design-led companies, not only understands the importance of how design and art can differentiate their business, but they make design a core competency. Business decisions aren't just made from crunching the numbers, they're also based on the emotional benefits of creative connection. This includes both product design and how the company designs customer experiences.

According to the Design Management Institute, this design-led philosophy is paying off. They tracked design-led companies against the S&P Index and reported that design-driven brands outperformed the index by 211 percent.[30]

In order to reach that level of success, design must be a core belief of everyone in your organization, especially your executive team.

A great example of this new type of CEO is the president of Mattel, Richard Dickson. He recently explained how their company is transforming to compete in the digital era by understanding what made their company great in the first place. And that beginning is all about creativity.

"Our founders thought of Mattel not as a toy company, but as a creations company. It was a great, American, started-in-a-garage company. That was design-led before anybody ever knew what that meant. Our founders weren't toy people. They were designers and inventors."[31]

Mattel understood the value of creative ideas from the start. They believed that the way to build and grow a business was all about creative ideas.

"The first big idea to come out of Ruth and Elliot Handler's garage wasn't a toy. It was a mindset. A conviction that taking bold risks on insightful and thoughtful and innovative ideas would delight children, and as a result, build a business. And it worked."

Another modern CEO who understands the importance of creating engaging content takes this idea even further. Gary Vaynerchuk, the energetic entrepreneur, author, and CEO of VaynerMedia, claims that every business better start creating entertaining content and holding their customer's attention or they risk becoming extinct.[32]

"Every single company out there, whether they know it or not, is a *media* company in addition to the business or product that they specialize in." He continues, "The faster your business realizes that it's a media company, the more likely it will be to succeed in 2020, in 2025, in 2030."[33]

That's a bold statement. It means that every company needs to understand that the way to succeed today is creating entertaining and emotional experiences. End of discussion. If you rely solely on the old way of doing business, by offering a great product and then simply sharing the benefits to your customers, you're sunk.

Rather, you need to use emotion to create experiences that hold your customer's attention, like a movie. And then continue to create compelling content that makes them feel something. Content that is entertaining and engaging. Only then will your customers stay loyal. These customer experiences aren't just marketing fluff.

One final example of this new change in mindset from big business leadership is Robert Lutz from GM. Daniel Pink describes his story.[34]

"GM hired a man named Robert Lutz to help turn around the ailing automaker. During his career, he's been an executive at each of the big three American automakers. He looks and acts like a marine, which he once was. He smokes cigars. He flies his own plane. He believes global warming is a myth peddled by the environmental movement.

"But when Lutz took over his post at beleaguered GM, and the *New York Times* asked him how his approach would differ from that of his predecessors, here's how he responded: 'It's more right brain... I see us being in the art business. Art, entertainment and mobile sculpture, which, coincidentally, also happens to provide transportation.'"

What we learn from these examples is that business is changing. The way to success is no longer just about great product development and number crunching. Consumers expect much more. They want amazing brand experiences. And these experiences require more than just a logical laundry list of product benefits and features.

To compete in this new era of business, you need to become an experience business. It's the next evolution from becoming a design-led company. Except the core requirement isn't just a belief in design. It's a belief in creating experiences that connect at an emotional level with people. It's ensuring that every decision in your company is focused on creating and delivering these emotional experiences. This certainly requires a transformation of not just your digital platforms, but a philosophical transformation of your leadership and employees.

No matter what company you work for, you are now in the art business. In the media business. In the emotion business.

Living in harmony.

I would venture to say that most of you reading this book have a deep-down belief that rational thought is still king. It's a concept that has been instilled in our brains from a young age. Do you feel that for any given problem, if you just slow down and really think about it in a logical way, you'll find the solution?

This deeply held belief isn't just a big part of our culture, it's a big part of business thinking. Years ago, while working at a regional advertising agency, I worked with an executive who'd say the same thing at the start of every project. "Hey guys," she'd say, "Before we try to solve this marketing problem, let's just slow down. Back up a bit. And let's think about this strategically." Her meaning was simple. Throwing creative ideas at a problem isn't the answer. If we slow down and just think rationally and tactically about the problem, we'll find the right solution.

More than just slowing down and thinking about it, many feel that our emotions can cloud our judgment. Which is why the philosophers of old felt we had to tame our emotions. We must strip ourselves of any emotions so they don't influence good thought.

Unfortunately, try as we might to stay purely logical, our emotions are deeply linked to our decisions. They're not separate. Logic and emotion are both connected in every decision we make. We can't have one without the other.

Logic isn't the great ruler in our brains. And we can't blame all mistakes on our emotions. If we rely solely only on logic for decisions, we simply won't be able to make them. Being human requires using emotions throughout the entire decision-making process. It's not just helpful in the discovery stage, but it's required all the way to deliberation and validation of a decision.

Our superiority over animals isn't that we can logically overpower our brain. Our superiority is that we are emotional beings.

Before you complain that I'm giving too much hate to logic, understand that I'm simply trying to give creativity an equal seat at the table. Remember, I'm a central brainer. I believe there is a need for both logical and creative ideas. But in my twenty-two years of experience in marketing, these two haven't been equals.

For centuries, logic has been elevated on a high pillar, and emotional ideas have been tossed aside as fluffy. But thanks to scientific discoveries in neuroscience, we know that humans literally can't make a decision with just logic. We need emotion. We need creative ideas.

Today, creative thought is no longer a side show. In our modern economy, it's becoming a major differentiator for businesses that hope to succeed. This is no longer just a rant from someone in your creative department, this is a topic that is top of mind for CEOs and thought leaders. Creative ideas are a major part of our economic future.

Logic isn't dead. The creative gut isn't dead. We need both.

Chapter 6

TWO SYSTEMS. ONE BRAIN.

66 A magician rehearses every bit of their act to make it look spontaneous. But improv has to be spontaneous and made to look like it's been rehearsed." —Bob Bedore[35]

Twenty-two years ago, Bob Bedore, was in a bad place. At least his business was. As the owner of a theater in Salt Lake City, Utah, he ran a reasonably successful operation that included both stand-up and traditional plays. But the theater often remained dark for weeks at a time in-between shows.

He needed a reliable filler that could bring in a regular audience at a moment's notice. As an actor himself, he finally decided to try something that he'd learned in training years earlier. Something that had never existed in the state. Or even in any nearby states. Bob decided to bring improv to Utah.

At this point in the state's history, people weren't familiar with improv. It hadn't become mainstream yet, and it was a struggle to get people to understand what it was and to make it viable. Improv theaters were only found in faraway locations like Chicago or the coasts.

So Bob started training actors and advertising his improv shows. At first, the shows were really just supposed to be a filler. But it soon became very apparent that the improv shows were outselling the plays. Bob no longer worried about the theater being dark. He now had a show that would light up his business for decades.

With this newfound success, Bob changed the name of the theater to "Quick Wits."

"Oddly enough, the name of the theater was a spontaneous decision. I said it would be a name we would use for now because it kind of describes instant comedy. I planned to come up with a better name later. But after 22 years I still haven't come up with a better name."[36]

Improv is a unique type of stand-up comedy. The actors are required to come up with characters, scenes, or dialogue in the heat of the moment. Often, they're given a few random suggestions from the audience, but most of the acting is off the cuff. The scene or action will change at a moment's notice. No two shows are ever the same.

This type of acting requires a unique set of skills. You can't rehearse. You have no idea what character you will be playing. All you can do is prepare for constant change.

Needless to say, those who are successful at improv have learned to think in a completely different way.

"I need actors who are team players. This may sound counter-intuitive, but I need people who are going to make the choices that make sense, not the choices that get laughs. They have to part of a team that's building a scene, rather than someone who's trying to get a laugh. The comedy will come. You can't force it, or it doesn't work.

"You have to have the ability to empty your brain and not think about anything. Then reboot your way of thinking instantly. You have to empty your brain and fill it up multiple times a minute. By being in the moment, you can feel what's coming up and be ready to bounce off the new thing that just came in. You can't get too far ahead of things. Things change quickly in improv. You may be thinking, OK, this scene I'm in right now is going great. Then boom, it changes. You have to start over and build up a new scene and be ready to stop on a dime and go a different direction."[37]

To those of us who are untrained in improv, this type of thinking can seem insane. How do you pay attention to the room and think logically about the rising action you have to build, and at the same time react instantly to new variables without seeming to think at all?

For those with experience in improv, the answer is easy. And doing it feels perfectly natural. Because they have trained themselves to switch seamlessly between their conscious and subconscious thinking.

That's what it all comes down to, the fact that we all have two different types of brain activity. Every one of us have two systems at play in our minds. One that helps us think logically and one that helps us react based on instinct. One is rational and the other is emotional.

To be great at improv, you have to master the logical variables in the scene with your conscious brain, and then trust in your training so that your subconscious mind can fill in all the gaps. These two systems of thought go much deeper than the simple connection between logic and emotion that we learned from Damasio. And once we understand how both systems work, we will understand what Bob Bedore is talking about.

Let's dig deeper into these two systems of thought.

Two points of view.

Since the late 1990s, hundreds of neuroscientists, psychologists, and behavioral economists have performed hundreds of experiments to learn more about the role of logic and emotion in our decisions.

"How can people be simultaneously so smart and so dumb?" Richard Thaler and Cass Sunstein ask in their book *Nudge: Improving Decisions about Health, Wellness, and Happiness.*

"Many psychologists and neuroscientists have been converging on a description of the brain's functioning that helps us make sense of these seeming contradictions. The approach involves a distinction between two kinds of thinking, one that is intuitive and automatic, and another that is reflective and rational."[38]

As discussed before, the brain may not always split cleanly into creative and rational halves, or even the frontal lobe and back of the brain. It's too interconnected and adaptable. That's why many scientists have stopped trying to compartmentalize sections of the brain, and instead talk about the overarching systems at work. As many see it, within our giant mess of neurons, there are two distinct functions. One that helps us with rational thought and another that provides emotional support. These two basic functions are the simplest way to explain how the brain works.

Here's a brief description of this breakthrough concept of two systems from Thaler and Sunstein. "The Automatic System is rapid and is or feels instinctive, and it does not involve what we usually associate with the word thinking. The Reflective System is more deliberate and self-conscious. One way to think about all this is that the Automatic System is your gut reaction and the Reflective System is your conscious thought."

Thaler and Sunstein call these two systems the Automatic System and the Reflective System. Where Daniel Kahneman in his book *Thinking, Fast and Slow* simply calls them System 1 and System 2.

For the purposes of this book, I'm going to use names for these two systems that feel less academic, since I'm writing more for a marketing and business audience, not psychologists. I'll refer to these two systems as our conscious and subconscious.

Our conscious function is easy to understand. It basically covers your awareness of the world around you. The alertness of speaking with another person. The day-to-day thoughts that are top of mind. The senses you're experiencing right now as you're reading this book. It's the knowledge of being alive.

Our subconscious is more mysterious. We know more is going on behind the scenes, but because we aren't always aware of it, it can be more difficult to comprehend. It's one of the great mysteries of life.

Your brain is performing a million tasks without you knowing about it. For example, your subconscious is directing your breathing and coordinating all those muscles and organs in order to stay alive. It's managing every little action within your body. Even more, it's processing millions of pieces of data coming in from your senses. Your vision alone is one of the most complex pieces of nature and requires a huge part of your brain's processing power.

And yet, we basically have no idea how it all works. It's a mystery. However, the subconscious is the playground where scientists are focusing a herculean effort today to better understand how our brains think.

The tip of the brainberg.

"Consciousness is just the tip of the iceberg; most of what goes on in your mind is hidden from you. As a result, your conscious experience can mislead you into thinking that our circuitry is simpler that it really is. Most problems that you experience as easy to solve are very difficult to solve—they require very complicated neural circuitry." —Leda Cosmides and John Tooby.[39]

This metaphor of the iceberg—even if somewhat clichéd—helps us grasp how these two systems work together. Your conscious thought, led by your prefrontal cortex, is the small section that floats above the water. You can see it. But it only handles a small part of our thinking.

Our subconscious is that massive chunk of grey matter under the water. We can't see it, but we know it's lurking underneath the surface—and it's vast compared to the part we can see.

But here's the interesting twist. Just because we can grasp our conscious, we assume it's doing the heavy lifting. After all, it's the one in charge, right? The truth is that the real thinking is being handled by our subconscious and the lightweight noodling is delegated to our conscious.

In the book *Incognito*, David Eagleman writes about the massive machine of the subconscious and how powerful it really is. He describes how the subconscious is more essential than we think, even though our conscious thoughts feel more important.

"To the extent that consciousness is useful, it is useful in small quantities, and for very particular kinds of tasks. It's easy to understand why you would not want to be consciously aware of the intricacies of your muscle movement, but this can be less intuitive when applied to your perceptions, thoughts, and beliefs, which are also final products of the activity of billions of nerve cells."[40]

Pause for a moment and imagine all the thinking that the subconscious has to handle for seemingly simple tasks. Like taking a single step as you walk. Imagine having to logically process every muscle, every tendon, every counterbalance as you move one foot out in front of you to take your full weight. If everything isn't in perfect order or balance, you would fall flat on your face. Yet humans do this effortlessly every day. And it's all being orchestrated by hundreds of impulses and drivers in your subconscious brain.

Or if we had to consciously think about making ourselves breathe. To focus on every muscle and molecule so that it worked in perfect harmony, every day, every second, we would either go crazy or mess everything up and die. Bad idea.

Instead, our subconscious calmly manages every aspect of keeping our bodies working. It's like a million little programs and computers inside, processing and calculating and ensuring that we go on living every day.

Because our conscious thinking is accessible, we assume it's more important. And more powerful. But in reality, our subconscious is the more dominant system. It handles all our mission-critical programs and regulates the functions that keep us alive. The systems that support life aren't up for micromanagement. They are safely regulated by our subconscious brain.

Our conscious brains only handle the simple things that aren't as critical. Like philosophy. Or rocket science. Or brain surgery. The stuff that doesn't kill us. The real thinking is going on beneath the surface.

It seems counter intuitive, but in reality, the easy thoughts to process are tasks that our conscious can handle. The job of our subconscious is much more neurally complex.

Our subconscious isn't a passive weak link. It powers more calculation and thought than we give it credit. Once we come to terms with the fact that our subconscious is more powerful than our conscious brain, we can learn to trust it. Just like the improv actors who work for Bob Bedore. Which hopefully means we can learn to use it more often for intuitive and creative thinking.

The strength of each system.

To really understand the differences of each system, it will take more than just imagining all the work our subconscious brain is doing. So let's explore a bit deeper into how much data your conscious and subconscious brain can handle.

Referring back to the metaphor of the brain as a computer, think of your conscious brain as the CPU or RAM. It can only hold a small amount of working memory. But the subconscious is much more robust. It's more like the hard drive. It can hold tons of applications and data.

One of the first studies that helped us understand the capacity of our RAM, or conscious brain, is a classic essay published by George A. Miller, a cognitive psychologist at Princeton University. His report from 1956 is called "The Magical Number Seven, Plus or Minus Two: Some Limits on our Capacity for Processing Information." In this essay, Miller built a case around the idea that our conscious mind can only hold an average of seven variables.

"Let me summarize the situation in this way," Miller explained. "There is a clear and definite limit to the accuracy with which we can identify absolutely the magnitude of a unidimensional stimulus variable. I would propose to call this limit the span of absolute judgment, and I maintain that for unidimensional judgments this span is usually somewhere in the neighborhood of seven.

"We are not completely at the mercy of this limited span, however, because we have a variety of techniques for getting around it and increasing the accuracy of our judgments. The three most important of these devices are (a) to make relative rather than absolute judgments; or, if that is not possible, (b) to increase the number of dimensions along which the stimuli can differ; or (c) to arrange the task in such a way that we make a sequence of several absolute judgments in a row."[41]

Miller studied the amount of data the average person can hold in their short-term memory. He based his report on many experiments by others in his field, as well as his own experiments. In one study, he measured how many random tones associated with a number people could hold in their conscious mind without mixing any of the tones or numbers up.

When a subject held only a few variables, they succeeded. As the variables moved beyond that magic number seven, people failed more often. The average for multiple experiments always landed on the same number of variables. His test subjects could only hold a few variables at a time in their conscious minds.

If you've ever taken a real IQ test, you've experienced something similar to Miller's test. And I'm not talking about those silly online IQ tests where they just give you trivia questions. In a legitimate IQ test, one of the exercises asks you to hold a stream of numbers in your head and repeat them back in reverse order. In the test, they keep adding one more number to the sequence of random numbers to see how many you can hold in your mind and correctly repeat back. It's quite challenging once you get past seven numbers. And only those with high IQ can hold longer sequences.

Miller also explained that we use other techniques to manage beyond seven variables, such as grouping variables into certain categories or recoding them into smaller chunks. This is why we often group phone numbers into sets of three or four.

Over the years, other researchers have challenged the number of variables established by Miller. Some feel that young adults are limited to three or four variables as their brains are still developing.[42] Or that this number changes over our lifetime and certainly each brain has different capacities.

In a more recent study by Nelson Cowan of the University of Missouri, Cowan presented research that shows how limits to our working memory is predictable at a capacity of closer to three to five chunks. He presented more sophisticated research that isolated our working memory by creating tests that would eliminate a person's ability to use grouping or structuring tactics.

According to Cowan, "In a broad sense, working memory ability varies widely depending on what processes can be applied to a given task. To memorize verbal materials, one can try to repeat them in one's mind (rehearse them covertly). One can also try to form chunks from multiple words. For example, to remember to buy bread, milk, and pepper, one can form an image of bread floating in peppery milk. To memorize a sequence of spatial locations, one can envision a pathway formed from the locations. Though we cannot yet make precise predictions about how well working memory will operate in every possible task, we can measure storage-specific capacity by preventing or controlling processing strategies."[43]

We can see practical applications of Cowan's estimate of three to five variables in current marketing situations. For example, on a web page, if we give more than five options in a global navigation, it can create choice overload and in user testing, people quickly become confused with too many navigation options. Or whenever we present campaigns to a group, if there are more than five concepts, it's very difficult for decision makers to weigh the options and remember the benefits of all campaigns at the same time. The sweet spot is three to five options.

But now that we understand that our conscious system can only hold a few variables, what about our subconscious?

A current study by the Salk Institute gives us a window into how much memory our brains can really hold.[44] They studied models of neurons where they attach to other neurons in areas called a synapse. Each neuron can have thousands of synapses that connect with thousands of other neurons. Electrochemical activity at each synapse is where signals travel and communicate throughout the brain.

By focusing on these micro-connections and measuring the amount of data that passes through, this new study estimates that each synapse is capable of handling more data than previously imagined, up to a factor of ten. And the Salk Institute discovered that the size of each synapse can adjust to fit the signal, which helps increase the amount of information it can communicate.

The amount of data that they estimate each individual synapse can hold is close to a petabyte of data. Because the memory capacity of a neuron is based on the size of its synapses, this discovery of more size categories increased our understanding of total capacity.

To put it into easy-to-understand terms, when you add up the numbers, this study suggests that our subconscious brains can hold a lot of data—like the equivalent amount as the entire Internet.

I'll repeat that so it sinks in. Our subconscious brains can hold the same amount of data as the entire Internet. Think about how much data that includes, especially when the amount of data in the cloud has been growing exponentially over the past few years. That includes every website. Every Facebook picture. Every YouTube video. Even the entire voice-over track of Zombo.com. That's an incredible amount of data.

Yet every human walking around on earth has that amount of space built in their heads. It's just hidden in our subconscious brain.

The contrast between the amount of information our rational brain and emotional brain can hold is striking. Five to seven variables compared to an entire Internet of data.

Our conscious aptitude isn't as powerful as we thought. In fact, our prefrontal cortex may control our conscious actions, but it still has limitations. It's just a limiting function of our biology.

In his book *How We Decide*, Jonah Lehrer wrote about the need to be cautious with placing too much stock in our prefrontal cortex. (Don't worry, I won't use any Dylan quotes.)

He writes, "The prefrontal cortex can handle only so much information at any one time, so when a person gives it too many facts and then asks it to make a decision based on the facts that *seem* important, that person is asking for trouble. We all need to know about the innate frailties of the prefrontal cortex so that we don't undermine our decisions."[45]

Many of us have experienced this when we have information overload. And this doesn't just happen when we have too many choices and freeze up, like with too many buttons on a website. Another great example is when you are presenting to a group. If you have too many slides in your presentation that are full of thick facts and deep data, it's only a matter of time before your audience is going to lose focus. So limit those sections of data to a handful of chunks or slides, and then add in more story to engage their subconscious brain. It's the same principle as breaking up a phone number into memorable chunks.

Of course, Lehrer also explains that our emotions aren't perfect either, but that by knowing about the limitations of both, we can make better decisions. What's important is knowing how each system works, both rational and emotional, so we can use both in the right way.

Holding a petabyte of data verses only five to seven variables is a key distinction between the two systems, but the speed at which they operate is even more important.

Different speeds for different jobs.

Our logical, conscious brain is slow. It requires deliberate thought and focus. We try to push out other distractions and really think about a problem. On the other hand, our emotional, subconscious system is extremely fast. It works with very little effort and feels as if thoughts come to us instantaneously.

Back to David Eagleman in *Incognito*, we get a wonderful description of the differences in the speed of these two systems.

"When trying to understand the strange details of human behavior, psychologists and economists sometimes appeal to a "dual-process" account. In this view, the brain contains two separate systems: one is fast, automatic, and below the surface of conscious awareness, while the other is slow, cognitive, and conscious. The first system can be labeled automatic, implicit, heuristic, intuitive, holistic, reactive, and impulsive, while the second system is cognitive, systematic, explicit, analytic, rule-based, and reflective."[46]

Eagleman also discusses a pivotal study by James McKeen Cattel in a paper titled "The time taken up by cerebral operations." At the time of the paper, nobody was thinking about the speed of thought, but his study was remarkably simple. He measured how quickly people react to questions based on the type of thinking required to answer the question. For example, he would include some questions that were direct and logical, like solving a math problem. And other questions pulled from emotions to get the right answer.

According to Eagleman, "Cattell's approach confronted the thinking problem head-on. By leaving the stimuli the same but changing the task (now make such-and-such type of decision), he could measure how much longer it took for the decision to get made. That is, he could measure thinking time, and he proposed this as a straightforward way to establish a correspondence between the brain and the mind."[47]

The results of this experiment help us understand that rational thought takes tens of milliseconds longer than an emotional response, which clocks in at a mere 160–190 milliseconds. And while measurements in milliseconds still seems pretty fast, when making a split-second decision, milliseconds can make the difference between success or failure.

Cattell's research concluded that logical decisions are slow and emotional decisions are fast. But there's an easier way for everyone to experience the difference in speeds between your fast and slow systems. The next section is a hands-on experiment you can try yourself.

A little test of your systems.

At this point in any conversation I have on the topic of fast and slow systems, many push back. They may say something like, "Yeah right, my fast system is my conscious system. I'm quick on my feet. I can come up with funny jokes and comments in a split second."

Just because you are aware of your conscious thinking doesn't mean it's faster than your emotions. Over the next few pages, I will give you a personal test where you can experience the two types of thinking for yourself.

To realize the full effect of this experiment, I need you to follow the instructions carefully when you flip from one page to the next. The reason is because this interactive experiment can be challenging when you, the reader, control the speed of flipping pages or reading words and numbers.

First, we will start with your slow system. On the following page is a math problem. As I can't measure how long it takes you to solve it, instead, I want you to pay attention to how long it takes you to complete it. Also, you need to complete each test without the help of any calculator or visual aid. Simply perform the calculations in your head to get a better sense of speed.

You can now flip to the next page.

Calculate the answer to the following:

$$247 + 331 = \underline{\hspace{3cm}}$$

When I ask this in person to a group, it usually takes about three to five seconds before someone shouts out the answer of 578.

The reality is that most of the others just give up. They think about it for a few seconds and it becomes too much. So they stop trying. Perhaps many of you did the same while reading this book and simply turned the page without completing the math problem.

Ok, that was perhaps too easy of a test for your slow system. Now let's try one that is a bit more challenging. One that's used in research to test your slow system.

This is called the *plus one*. Here's how it works. I show you a series of random numbers and give you a few seconds to memorize them. Then I remove the numbers so you can't see them. All you need to do is add one to each number in the sequence. So a number 2 becomes a 3. And a 7 becomes an 8. Then repeat back the entire sequence with the new numbers.

Seems simple, right? The only issue with us not doing this in person in a lab is that you will need to only look at the series of numbers on the next page for a second or two before turning the page again, or simply closing your eyes and repeating back the new series of numbers. To get a real sense of this test, I encourage you to try your best to calculate all this in your head without looking at the numbers on the page when you do it.

So here we go. Flip the page, take a second to memorize the sequence, and then close your eyes and add one digit to each number.

Add one digit to each number in this sequence:

4397583

Now close your eyes.

How long did it take you to complete the challenge?

For most of us, it takes an incredible amount of effort just to complete the problem. The good news is that you are not alone.

When people are asked to try this challenge, here's what happens. Their eyes dilate. Their hands sweat. They try to shut out the rest of the world and really focus on the problem. Everything slows down. They use up a lot of energy and feel tired after. In essence, they have to focus all their energy on their logical brain and ignore everything else.

And just imagine if the sequence of numbers is greater than seven digits. With just a few variables—like the number of 268—you could easily handle this challenge. But if the sequence is eight or ten variables, it becomes extremely difficult.

And the truth is, when I do this experiment in presentations, I see people's faces wrinkle up, their eyes roll back, and after several seconds, they just give up. It's too hard and takes too long.

You've just experienced your slow system in action.

Now let's move on to your fast system.

Over the next few pages, I'm going to show you an image or a single word. Here's what I want you to do. The moment you see the image or word, I want you to think of all the memories or ideas that enter your mind. And I want you to see how fast those thoughts or memories are communicated to your conscious mind.

With this experiment, I'm not worried about how fast you're turning the page. But to get a real sense of the speed and depth, once you see an image, pause for just a moment so you can experience how fast you feel something after seeing the word or image.

Clear your head. Relax. And now turn the page.

What emotions did you experience? For some, thoughts of cuddly kittens are highly emotional. That's why we have so many cat posters and animated GIFs of cats all over the web. For others, a picture of a cat brings up feelings of disgust. Either way, did you sense any past memories or experiences involving a cat?

And did you notice how fast those emotions and ideas were communicated?

Let's try one more experiment. When you're ready, turn the page. And again, pay attention to all the emotions and thoughts you feel.

I'm not sure what thoughts came to mind, but I know that this moment in time was so impactful for so many people. Many of us remember exactly where we were standing when we heard the news. We know the people who watched the news coverage with us. We can recall many distinct details of that day.

Without dwelling too long on September 11, 2001, the point is that our subconscious can communicate to us through emotions in an extremely fast and efficient way. In a matter of microseconds, a ton of information can be communicated through feelings.

This is your fast system in action.

Two systems in under two seconds.

The concept of a slow logical brain versus a lightning-fast emotional brain is nowhere more apparent than it is in improv. There are times when you need to use your fast, emotional brain and times when you must rely on your slow, rational system.

"You have to live in the moment, not in your head," said Bob when explaining both systems. "What's happening right now in this exact moment—that's what's important. In improv, there's a mixture of having to think both logically and emotionally. Logically, I need to know what's the next thing that's happening? You have to be paying attention to where things are going, what the emcee is throwing at you, and you have to follow the rules of the game.

"But improv isn't really acting, it's reacting. So emotionally, you have to respond to whatever just happened, or whatever new stimulus has just been brought to your attention. You have to react to that. So, I'm never thinking three reactions, or even two reactions ahead. I'm just flowing and responding instantly to what's happening right now. Sometimes, all I'm really thinking about is surviving the scene."

Improv actors have to use both systems at the same time. But to be great, to really get the audience excited, they have to have lightning-fast responses. And that means relying on their expertly trained improv brains to succeed. Without all the past experiences and practice, they won't have the quick wit to bring down the house.

In many situations, you use your fast, subconscious mind without knowing it. When you use your subconscious to rely on a feeling of what to do, you're really tapping into hundreds of previous decisions and similar situations that you've practiced before. Just like an improv performer.

For Bob, understanding both ways of thinking isn't just essential for training new performers. It's important to know how the audience is thinking as well. A great show pulls both logic and emotion.

The audience knows the rules of each game and logically understands the variables that the host adds to the scene. But they also enjoy the discovery and pleasure of the quick, emotional connections that the actors and actresses add. The journey of the audience with the performers from logic to emotion is what creates an engaging experience. An unexpected experience they are willing to pay for again and again.

This is as important for us as it is for Quick Wits in creating memorable brand experiences. Because we can't lose sight of why we're discussing logic and emotion and the two systems of the brain. It all relates back to making the best creative experiences for your brand or company.

The key takeaway for now is that we have two systems. Our conscious and subconscious. And that they both work at different speeds performing different jobs. Our conscious thought is slow and deliberate, leading the charge and guiding our actions. Our subconscious thought is fast and flexible, handling most of the legwork without us knowing how.

Now that we recognize the two systems and know how differently they work, the next chapter helps us understand how our conscious and subconscious work together in making decisions. And we'll discuss the different types of decisions that are best suited for each system.

Chapter 7

HOW WE MAKE DECISIONS

Imagine for a moment that you're sitting in your car. You've just finished up a long day at work and you're ready for a break. You just want to get home, eat some dinner, and relax. You start the engine and pull out into traffic.

And then suddenly you're home.

You don't remember making any conscious decisions about driving. You were lost in your thoughts and your subconscious basically drove you home without any input. You've just experienced your brain on autopilot.

Sometimes this can be a bit scary. You may ask yourself, "What if I don't pay attention at an intersection and I cause an accident?"

But the truth is that you *were* paying attention. Your mind was actively engaged with steering the wheel perfectly as you changed lanes. You came to a stop at a stoplight. You did everything right.

Now, let's take that same scenario but with a slight variation. You're driving home on autopilot, deep in thought. But halfway home, you see an accident up ahead. There are flashing police lights and perhaps an ambulance or a fire truck.

As you approach the accident, suddenly time slows down. You twist your neck like any good rubbernecker while trying to get a good view of the smashed car, or to see if the people are ok. As you pass the accident, you're very aware of your driving and of every little detail in the moment.

This second example is a very different experience. You're consciously aware of the entire experience, especially if you see something shocking or unique.

This happens because our brains are designed to detect anomalies. Think of the massive amount of data that inundates your brain through all your senses. As you drive, your eyes are recording every frame of every moment. Your nose is smelling and filtering. Your ears are noticing the hum of the engine.

As we've discussed, the subconscious logs all of this data. But there's no possible way your conscious mind can process it all. After all, it can only hold a few variables at a time, right? So the subconscious takes it all in and only notifies the prefrontal cortex or your conscious brain if there's something new. Something that doesn't match your previous experiences.

This goes back to speed and efficiency. The brain has to be efficient. It runs on such a small amount of electrical power that it can't afford to keep all the lights on all the time. It can't process and retain everything. (For the record, the brain runs on ten to twenty watts of power, barely enough to run a dim light bulb.)[50]

Instead, like an NSA agent listening in on all our phone calls, the subconscious sifts through all the incoming data and only acts on the anomalies—the inputs that are different or unique. Only when it finds an anomaly does it notify the conscious brain.

In our example, you only notice something on the drive home when it doesn't fit the typical experience. An accident. A new billboard. Something out of place. Only then does your slow conscious brain fire up and you attend to all the details. That's when time slows down as you pass the accident because your slow system has been activated.

Dr. Scott Steffensen, a neuroscientist at Brigham Young University, explained to me how our brains predict the world around us. Awareness of our world only happens when something violates our predictions.

"When our brain is doing its job at predicting our surroundings, our subconscious is in control," Steffensen said. "Only when there is an error or something doesn't match our predicted reality, does the conscious brain kick in. Only then do we become aware and notice the element that's different."[51]

The way our brains remain efficient is by only keeping the required amount of data and predicting the rest. As we drive home, we don't need to analyze every street sign or tree because we've already seen it. Our brains anticipate that stop sign and let us know it's there—by automatically engaging our foot on the brake petal. Even when you didn't consciously look at the sign and decide to stop.

This process of predicting is hardwired into our brains. Literally.

Erik Du Plessis, in his book *The Advertised Mind*, offers insight into how our subconscious is wired to feed predicted information to our conscious mind rather than the other way around.

"There are more dendrites leading from the limbic area in the brain towards the frontal lobes than there are dendrites leading the other way. In other words, there is more information flowing from the area of emotion towards the area of rationality than there are dendrites feeding back into the system that generates our emotions."[52]

Nowhere is this story of how our brains predict our environment more apparent than with our visual cortex. The visual cortex creates a model of our world and only adds new data in small amounts. Our eyes aren't recording everything we see in front of us. Our visual cortex only records a small window, and our memory fills in the rest of the picture.

Here's how Dr. Steffensen explained it,

"Your vision input is about the equivalent of an Ethernet port. About 10 to 100 megabits per second. That information is flowing in, but you can't attend to all of it. You only attend to a little narrow amount called the "searchlight" of your world. Your searchlight is actually a very small bit. Yet you're having a lot of information come in your brain, visually, auditory, touch, etc. But you only attend to the small amount that matters. What we perceive is what matters.

"Perception is weird and fascinating. It's one of the things that separate us from animals. We're making up stuff all the time. Your vision right now is creating data because there's not information coming in from certain parts of your retina. Your brain literally makes it up. Your brain somehow fills in all the gaps. A lot of our senses work that way."[53]

This is important because it means our executive function isn't a dictator. It doesn't tell the rest of the brain all the information that should be turned into a memory. Instead, it only deals with the anomalies. It only finds the mistakes in the predictions and tries to correct it with new data.

The subconscious does the heavy lifting with predicting the world around us and only alerts the CEO if there's a problem. This is how we learn and understand our surroundings without overwhelming our minds with too much new data.

Anomaly detection is not only important in warning us of danger, it also helps us compare new experiences with old ones—helping us make better decisions. Which brings us to an important crossroads. As we are making decisions, what happens when our subconscious finds a match within our database of old memories, and what does our brain do when there isn't a match?

We have a match.

Before the subconscious alerts the conscious system about an anomaly, it has already performed some legwork. It has already done a massive cross analysis of all the existing memories on the hard drive. Like a Google search, it has checked all the results to make sure there isn't something already recorded in the help database.

If any of the top results are a match, then it sends a message that we've already experienced this before. The way our subconscious notifies the conscious is with a burst of emotion or neurochemicals. Our subconscious sends us back an emotional trigger, reminding us of the previous decision.

Imagine, for a moment, if you've experienced the following emotions:

"Don't touch the fire, it will hurt, remember." Or, "Yes, you liked that experience eating cookies, you can feel good about doing that again."

In 1999, professor John Allman, a neuroscientist at the California Institute of Technology, discovered another insight into why we react so quickly to anomalies. He and his colleagues discovered a new type of neuron that is only found in humans and other great apes.[54]

These special neurons are called spindle neurons because of their distinct shape. Most neurons are short and have many dendrites. Dendrites are the short branches or extensions of the cell that communicate with other neurons through neurochemicals. Spindle neurons are much longer and have only a single dendrite. We'll get into more details about how neurons work in the next chapter. For now, it's just important to know that spindle neurons are unique.

The unique function of these long spindle neurons is that they're intertwined around the brain, allowing rapid communication. They are considered "air traffic controllers" for emotions by bringing signals from deep into the brain to the distant outer parts.

One of the main regions where we find the largest amount of spindle neurons is in the Anterior Cingulate Cortex (ACC). The ACC is tasked with error detection and controls motivation to act, heart rate, and blood pressure. The ACC is also a messenger from the amygdala, transmitting intense emotions quickly to our frontal cortex. In other words, it quickly notifies your conscious when there is an anomaly or a match from a previous experience.

Once a match is made, these long spindle neurons can quickly increase our heart rate and blood pressure. By releasing a small amount of neurochemicals like dopamine, these unique and powerful spindle neurons can instantly flood our brain and notify our conscious mind that something needs our attention. This exchange is what makes our emotional brain so fast. We don't have to start with an emotion in one small area of the brain, but we can instantly flood the entire brain with emotion.

Our brain creates subtle patterns with dopamine levels based on all our past successes and failures. Even a small fluctuation in our neurochemical levels can instantly alert our subconscious that there is an anomaly, even if we can't consciously see it. But we can feel it. These small changes in dopamine can create big emotions.

Think back to the experiment in the previous chapter about our fast system. When you saw an image or a word, you received an instant flood of memory without having to use your prefrontal cortex to analyze it. No need to processes anything with logic. You just feel it.

When there isn't a match.

But the brain doesn't detect anomalies just to attract the attention of the prefrontal cortex and remind us of past memories. It has a secondary motivation. It's how we learn and grow. When the brain ingests a bit of information that's never been recorded, it doesn't know what to do with it. The brain scans through all the folders of the hard drive, checking for a match. Or at least something similar.

When it can't find an answer, it notifies the CEO *not* because it wants to reject the new data, but because it needs direction of where and how to file it away for the future. Our brains want to learn. Create new memories. Make new decisions.

That doesn't mean that the CEO is going to do the actual work of making the decision. Holistically, the CEO couldn't possibly handle every decision, but needs to be the great manager. It doesn't have the time, energy, or even capacity to handle it all.

What the CEO actually acts on depends on the type of decision. More often than not, the CEO delegates down to the subconscious to continue working on the problem until an answer is found.

Again, we can learn from the ACC. As it helps control error prediction, it not only alerts us when there's an anomaly, but it also helps regulate our emotions through trial and error.

This is how we learn, by recognizing errors and reminding our conscious to take the correct action. If our brain recognizes the hot flame, it will send a quick feeling to avoid a certain action. This is how we avoid repeating mistakes. But if it's a new experience, like green flame instead of orange, the subconscious needs a little help from the CEO to analyze the new data.

Once our brain is aware of the anomaly, it's time to make a decision and learn a lesson. After analyzing the data and emotions from similar experiences, our brain makes a decision and locks it in by burning a new memory trace into our long-term memory.

And the way we send decisions back to our long-term memory is the same way we receive messages—through emotions. We feel good about a decision.

But why an emotion? Why not simply send back a logical data point?

For several reasons. First, because emotions are extremely fast while conscious processing is much slower. Our brains need to learn quickly, and with the hardware already in place, it makes sense to use that high-speed emotional connection. By using the instantaneous speed of emotion, our long-term memory and executive function are able to stay in sync.

Another reason is the fact that we learned from Damasio's patients—that without emotions, we aren't able to lock in a decision. It's this two-way street that allows us to learn from the past and adjust for the future in a split second. Otherwise we have to start from scratch and make new decisions without the instant access to our old decisions.

Dr. Steffensen explained this process with a simple adage. "'Neurons that fire together, wire together.' In other words, the more activity you have in a certain pathway, the more it becomes plastic. And that plasticity is mediated by certain neurotransmitters and chemicals—also known as the regulators of emotion. So when we make a decision, our brains are flooded with feelings."[55]

We use emotion to remind us of past decisions and create new memories because that's how the brain works. The neurochemicals that help our neurons communicate result in our emotions. Dopamine, oxytocin, serotonin—all our neurochemicals create our emotions of pride, pleasure, and fear.

This emotional super highway is the brain's way of maintaining sanity and quickly making millions of decisions from the millions of data points that are flooding in from all our input devices.

In marketing, we often talk about the thousands of messages consumers see every day from advertising. But in reality, those thousands of advertising messages are nothing compared to the massive amounts of data that our brains deal with every second.

Consider again the act of seeing one frame of vision with our eyes. There are millions of data points representing each pixel of light flooding into our minds. Each pulse has to be processed and summarized into a picture. And where our eyes don't focus, our brains fill in the picture by estimating what we would be seeing based on millions of other images that have been created in our brains. It's not surprising perhaps that nearly a third of our brains are devoted just to vision.

Then compare that to the most powerful photo manipulation software on the market, Adobe Photoshop. It's an amazing solution, and Adobe engineers are constantly adding new features that seem magical. Like adjusting the perspective of the image to a location where the photographer could never stand. Or automatically changing a photo from daytime to a night scene. Or instantly logging metadata about a photo based on common pixel proximity. These Photoshop features use incredible algorithms and data logic to function. Yet everyone's eyes do all this and more, without any logical thought.

Today we talk about Big Data, and most companies know how we can easily become inundated with too much data if we don't know how to process it. Fortunately, our brains know how to process massive amounts of data. Otherwise we would have to logically start over at ground zero on every decision with the slow processes of the prefrontal cortex.

And all this analysis is communicated to your conscious with a simple blip of emotion. It's actually quite amazing if you pause to think about it. Every little emotion isn't just a base animal instinct that we need to overcome. Rather, each emotion represents a massive amount of analysis, process, and decision making.

Emotions represent an extreme amount of rational thought. They just happen to be processed in our subconscious. Unfortunately, we often act as if this is second-class thinking. But it's not.

The next time you feel an emotion, take a moment to think about all the data that was instantly communicated to your conscious mind. Because that single emotion is really the equivalent of innumerable rational thoughts.

Chapter 8

DECISIONS. DECISIONS. DECISIONS.

Picture a busy downtown street in a large city. You're in a central plaza, with sky scrapers on all sides, shading the square. Hundreds of business men and women rush past each hour without looking you in the eyes. You don't mind because you're one of them. Stopping to chat would only slow you down. You're on your way to lunch and you've only got thirty minutes before you need to be back for a meeting.

As you hustle along, you spot a man panhandling in the middle of the square. You try to avoid him, but the flow of the crowd pushes you past him. He's sitting perfectly still on a set of wide steps, holding a stick and wearing sunglasses. He has placed a small bowl with a few coins on the concrete in front of him, next to a sign that reads, "I'm blind. Please help."

You walk past him every morning on your way to work, and again every evening on your way home. You rarely stop because you never carry cash.

Then one morning, something changes. You notice another man dressed in a brown sport coat with patches on the elbows. He has stopped in front of the blind man. He picks up the piece of cardboard and pulls a sharpie out of his jacket pocket.

He writes something on the sign and places it back on the ground. He walks away without saying a word. You raise your eyebrow in interest but continue walking without missing a step. Soon the mystery man is lost in the crowd.

That evening as you walk by, you notice something different. People are stopping to drop money in the bowl. As you get closer, you see that the bowl is now completely full. You're amazed, so you decide to see what the strange man wrote on the sign. As you step close to pause and read the sign, the blind man raises his head in your direction. He senses that someone has stopped near his sign.

You reach into your pocket and pull out a dollar bill. In a gruff voice, the beggar asks, "Please, can you read to me my sign? I don't know what it says."

As you bend down to drop the dollar into the bowl, you read the sign out loud, "It's spring. I'm blind. Please help."

Emotion and memory.

This story has been told and retold for decades as an example of how great writing can make all the difference. It's been the narrative of several award-winning short films in a variety of film festivals. It's been a commercial for a marketing firm. It's basically one of those stories in marketing that has become folklore.

Many in advertising have credited the story to one of the original mad men, David Ogilvy, because he used it in his 1985 book *Ogilvy on Advertising* to illustrate the effectiveness of good copywriting.[56] But it seems that Ogilvy wasn't the author. He was simply inspired by the American poet David Kirby, who wrote *On My Mother's Blindness*, where he describes another poet, Jacques Prévert.[57] At least at the time of this writing, Prévert is generally thought to be the original scribe in the story.[58] In Prévert's 1977 version, the sign actually reads "Blind man without a pension." The passing man then alters the text to read, "Spring is coming, but I won't see it.["]59

The reason I share this story is to illustrate a point about how we remember ideas. The story of the blind man's sign is one that many people in the marketing industry share as a classic story of the power of good writing. They remember it because it's packed with emotion.

The slight change to the message, in just a few words, creates an emotional hook. The word spring makes us think of a variety of good things, such as rebirth, growth, flowers, sunshine and life. Knowing that the blind man won't be able to experience this makes us feel empathy for his situation. We feel that deep emotion of loss and sadness that others are missing out. That's why the others passing by were moved to donate some extra change.

And that same emotion is why that story has continued to live in our collective minds for decades.

The reason stories like this last for so long is because of the way we remember. And before we get into the details of how we lay down a memory track, the big takeaway on this topic is that emotion plays a big part on how strong our memories will be and how easy they are to remember.

That's because when a strong emotion is present when we create a new memory track, it has a higher chance of being burned into our long-term memory.

As Dr. Larry Cahill from the University of California, Irvine, said, "Why do you remember things and why do you forget things? The thing that really sculpts memory. The thing that really helps control your memory is *emotion*."60

How we remember.

The act of saving a memory on our hard drive, or long-term memory is called encoding. Here's how it works.

Our brains are made of billions of neurons that have many small branches called dendrites and one long tentacle called an axon. These extensions interconnect with other neurons as they send and receive electrochemical signals. At the tips of all these branches are small receptors called a synapse, where the electrical or chemical connections are made between two neurons.

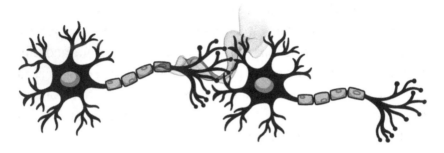

As you can imagine, with billions of neurons and each neuron having hundreds or thousands of synapses, the entire brain has a massive amount of small connection points.

When you lock in a memory, in essence, a series of neurons and synapse connections fire an electrochemical signal in a certain pattern, like a circuit or a pathway. As the pattern is created, each synapse is conditioned to fire and repeat that same pattern. Think of it as something similar to muscle memory. The chain reaction is made and the more it is fired, the stronger the pattern or memory becomes.[61]

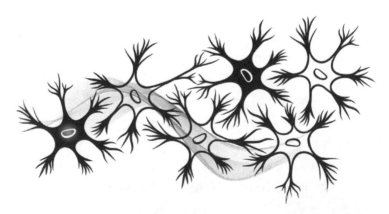

An example is when you choose a favorite color. The first time you decide you like that color, you lock it in with an emotional memory trace. At first, it's a weak decision. But the more you reinforce that decision over and over, you can remember it more easily. Years later, you feel confident about your favorite color.

The process of firing these patterns is based on the presence of neurochemicals at each synapse in the circuit. The more we repeat that pattern, the more neurochemicals like dopamine are released, and the stronger the pattern or memory becomes.

And since these neurochemicals are expressed in our brains as emotions, we can see how important a role emotion plays in making memories. The more emotional the situation, the more chemicals are released, the greater chance we can create a strong memory pattern.

Back to our computer analogy, it's like we are burning ones and zeros in a pattern on a disc. That pattern of on and off switches can be read back to give us a data point. Only in our brains, it's a series of synapses that are firing neurochemicals to create the pattern. Our memories are simply ones and zeros until we associate them with a burst of emotion. Once the pattern of emotion is established, that's when they become a memory. And since our brains have a seemingly limitless amount of connections, we can burn down tracks that hold vast amounts of data.

Once a memory track is created, our ability to recall it is based on the strength of the track. Perhaps the memory was created when we weren't paying enough attention and the track is weak. Or we haven't fired that particular pattern in a while. So the track may still be strong, but we are just having trouble finding and retrieving it.

The good news is that the brain does a tremendous job of making sure important memories are recorded. In fact, sometimes the brain creates parallel memories in different locations.[62] For example, usually our memories are cemented in our long-term memory by an area called the hippocampus. The hippocampus helps consolidate information from short-term memory to long-term memory. It guides the creation of the memory patterns.

But sometimes, during a highly emotional or traumatic event, another area of the brain, the amygdala, also creates a memory track. These memories are difficult to forget, and they often return to our conscious, even when we don't want them to. Like in cases of veterans who experience PTSD.[63]

This is important to note, because it means that our brains are dynamic and can create two separate instances of the same memory during emotionally charged experiences. It's like having a backup of your hard drive of memories.

Another exciting insight is that our brains also retain memories even if we have trouble recalling them. The *Journal of Nature* featured an MIT study where scientists stimulated certain brain cells using a new technology known as optogenetics.[64]

They've isolated specific cells in the hippocampus of mice and have learned how to manipulate these cells by activating existing memories, altering emotional associations, or even planting false memories. (That's right, science fiction may be more real than you think.) By stimulating certain cells, they were able to trigger and bring back lost memories in rodents with amnesia.

"The important point is, this a proof of concept. That is, even if a memory seems to be gone, it is still there. It's a matter of how to retrieve it," says Susumu Tonegawa, the senior author of the study and director of the RIKEN-MIT Center for Neural Circuit Genetics.[65]

Helping customers remember.

Of course, even if the conditions are perfect and we've communicated an emotionally packed message, that alone won't determine success. There are other elements that can minimize our chances of connecting with a customer.

Remember, encoding is one part of the process. Other factors such as physical brain damage or problems with retrieval can inhibit recall of the memory.

Even with a perfectly functioning brain, we have to realize the limitations of big data. With so many messages and inputs from our surroundings, our minds can't focus on everything. Sometimes our attention is dealing with so many anomalies that we have to play favorites.

Dr. Carmen Simon, a cognitive scientist and founder of Rexi Media, explains that most humans forget 90 percent of what you show them.[66] Even when we try to pay attention, we can't focus on everything at the same time, so some things will fade. She encourages us to embrace this fact and do our best to make sure that customers at least retain the most important 10 percent.

We start by asking ourselves what is the most important thing that our audience needs to remember. Then we craft our messages and marketing in a way that guides our customers to remember those key facts.

In a similar vein, when reviewing a creative brief, I've often used the analogy of the bed of nails. If you try to cram too many ideas into the "key message" or "single statement" it weakens the message. When you lounge on a bed of nails, nothing gets through. But if you only have one nail, it's going to get your attention.

We sometimes called this the philosophy of restraint. We need to be crystal clear with what we are asking of our customers. And we need the strength to avoid putting too many messages that only create brain soup.

Many of us are guilty of this in marketing. Our simple messages turn into a long run-on sentence with a half dozen conjunctions and subordinate clauses. This is especially true when a committee is trying to create a value statement as a group.

Instead, we need to have the intestinal fortitude to limit our message to a simple idea. It's our way of understanding the limitations of our brains and giving our marketing the best possible chance of success.

This does not mean we should revert to straightforward facts. There is a balance here. We need to be crystal clear *and* emotionally rich in our messages. That's the magic—the perfect balance of art and science.

The best way to stack the odds in our favor is to do both. If we want our audience to remember, we need to light up their brains with emotionally charged ideas that have a better chance of locking in a memory track. And to avoid overstimulation, we do this by logically focusing our message on that 10 percent we want them to remember. The anomalies.

This requires insight and restraint. It doesn't require a ton of boring messaging. Sometimes, all it takes is just a few words. Like the phrase "It's spring" added to the blind man's sign.

Because the name of the true author of that story may fade with history. But the emotional memory of the story will always live in our minds.

Chapter 9

THE ANSWER IS BOTH

One of the applications I use the most on my laptop is the built-in calculator. It's a basic app that comes standard on the latest smartphones and computers.

And most of the time, the calculator app is quite simple. It has a standard nine-key setup and handles basic calculations like addition and multiplication. Few of us ever download a more complex calculator to figure out the tangent of a plane curve or the square root of a large number. Most of us just need the calculator to figure out pretty simple problems.

The calculator comes standard because it's super useful for everyday decisions. Like adding up a list of expenses for a budget. Or figuring out how much tax I'll have to pay if I buy a new microwave.

The calculator app hardly uses the maximum computing power of our devices. In fact, it takes very little power from the CPU. You can buy a simple calculator at a corner store with the most basic transistors and a mini battery that will last for years. Because the calculator doesn't require much power or circuitry.

Yet I use the calculator all the time. Because it can hold more variables and often arrives at an answer faster than me trying to calculate it in my head.

Of course, the calculator app isn't the only reason I have a laptop or smartphone. I use the latest tech to solve other problems and needs. I may push the limits of my laptop when editing video in Premier Pro, where the files are large and I need to maximize the output of the CPU. Or I may have dozens of open applications when I design or write, and I'm constantly switching from one app to the next.

The reality is that I have a variety of needs. And the best way to solve each need is with the right application for the job. A quick math problem is best solved with the simple calculator. But a complex adjustment to a photo is best solved with Photoshop.

The same is true when we are making decisions or creating new memories. Our brains may be a complex machine with massive computational power. But there are certain decisions that are better handled by our slow, conscious system, and some that need to rely on our fast, subconscious system.

When we compare the two systems of computation power in our brains—our conscious and our subconscious—one isn't superior for all choices. The answer isn't that we should try to be rational and logical with every choice. Or that we should rely only on our emotions to survive. We need both. And we should use the strengths of both systems in everyday life.

Remember, our conscious can roughly hold Miller's seven (plus or minus two) variables at a time, while our subconscious is practically limitless. This is important to keep in mind when we consider the many decisions we need to make in a marketing context.

In basic terms, if we're asking a customer to think about a relatively simple thing, like a math problem, or we are asking them to compare a few simple features of a straightforward product, then appealing to their conscious brain is ideal. Like a spatula, the

115

variables may be simple and only include the handle or color or the material it's made from. In these situations, our logical brain can calculate value rather quickly. It's like a calculator, and it can handle it.

But if our marketing decision must break through the clutter of messages and it's a more complex choice like buying a house, or it has hundreds of variables and product options like a new car, then an emotional appeal may be the better option. These decisions require a supercomputer, like a modern laptop.

In reality, most of the choices consumers have to make are pretty difficult and include a mix of simple and complex choices. That's when our little CEO requires the help of the entire company and taps into the super computer under the iceberg.

Which means the real answer of whether to use logic or emotion in your marketing is to use *both*. Consumers use both systems in making decisions, so we need to plan for both in our marketing campaigns.

Right now, I'm sure your logical half is nodding and thinking, "See, I knew it. All this talk about embracing emotions is situational." That's not what I'm saying. The point is that too often with business and marketing decisions, we are *only* using logic. And now that we know how emotions work in the brain, we need to start swinging the pendulum back to the middle and embracing more emotion in marketing decisions.

The advice is simple. Don't go all in with just one half. Too often as marketers we live in the extremes.

For decades agencies and marketers have battled over the role of logic and emotion in marketing. It's been creative versus strategy. Brand versus direct marketing. And art versus science.

What we need is an equal seat at the table for both sides. However, just like my opening story with Russell, many business leaders have learned in their MBA degrees to only focus on the numbers, the logical patterns, and the risks.

But when business leaders think that emotional marketing is fluffy and unnecessary, then they don't understand how humans think.

If you want to avoid risk, look at our biology. If you want a sure bet on your marketing dollars, then you need to embrace a balance of both logic *and* emotion.

We are biased from history, from our schooling, from culture, and from best practices in business to discount the emotional side of advertising. But when you look deep into the science, the type of marketing that will better connect with customers, that will help them create positive memories with your brand, and that will turn your messages into money is marketing that has a foundation of emotion.

Many companies are realizing the need for this balance, and we are seeing new positions at the highest levels where creativity and design have a seat at the table. Like chief experience officer or chief design officer. But those progressive companies are the exception. We need business leaders who understand the value of emotion and put a premium on business decisions that give creativity a voice.

More often than not, this means understanding the value of creative ideas in a sea of data and logic.

Data and your gut instincts.

Data-driven marketing is misunderstood. On a recent LinkedIn thread in a discussion about the need for creative ideas, one business leader said that we don't need creative ideas anymore because we have this. Then he pasted a link to a small digital analytics company.

His point was that we have more ways to measure customer choices than ever before. We know what customers like and what they click on, so therefore we don't need creativity to lure them into a purchase. We can simply present the data and the customer will make the right choice.

I've also read many other articles on this topic where some claim that the marketing gut is dead. We no longer have to guess anymore. We have data.

Whenever I come across these types of arguments, it makes me smile. Because I work for one of the most sophisticated analytics companies in the world. (According to independent analysts like Gartner.)[67]

At Adobe, we understand the relationship between data and creativity. Our company is built on the platform that art and science should live in harmony. Data doesn't remove the need for creativity. Rather, data helps you understand the customer, so you can deliver creative experiences.

With the most advanced analytics, the best you can hope for is to surface an anomaly or insight that you can instantly act on. But you still need the creative idea to create a relevant and emotional experience.

Algorithms can offer you suggestions from holistic customer data. It can bring anomalies to the forefront with fantastic data visualization. It can make statistical suggestions based on similar customers and we can use artificial intelligence to serve up the right data at the most opportune moment to make an informed marketing decision.

But it won't replace your intuition. It won't make the leap to a new innovation on its own. It's the base. The catalyst. The yin to your intuition yang.

Why does it always have to be an either/or equation? Why take a scarcity approach?

The truth is that it doesn't have to be. Both data and our gut are critical to business success. There's plenty of room at the business table to comfortably seat both creativity and science. It's not about one versus the other. In order to survive in today's economy, you need both.

Because the best way to know your customer is to bring together all your data sources. This includes your company's first-party database. And any secondary or third-party data that you can buy. And you should add in all your personal experience data, or marketing gut, so you have all sources of data to make the best decision possible.

When you think of your marketing gut as another source of data, should you toss this out just because you have a digital method for collecting more data? No chance.

If you want your business to succeed, you need to invest in both digital data and human experience. You need both logic and emotion to create the most amazing brand experiences.

And this isn't just my personal opinion. Recently, a team of scientists from several universities conducted research to better understand what situations are better for logical deliberation or trusting your emotions.

In a report titled, *Should I go with my gut? Investigating the benefits of emotion-focused decision making*, Joseph A. Mikels, Andrew E. Reed, Sam J. Maglio, and Lee J. Kaplowitz began with the premise that logical or deliberative thinking has historically been considered the best way to make a sound decision. People usually hold all the factors in memory and deliberate over them to reach the best decision.

They mentioned that past studies had introduced the idea that for complex decisions, we should rely on our emotions or gut. And for simple choices with only a few variables, our logical brain is more ideal. So they wanted to prove it out and see if this is true.

They concluded that for complex decisions, listening to your emotions is actually a very effective strategy for making good decisions. Here's an excerpt of their final summary:

"While many open questions remain, the current results support the notion that when the going gets tough, go with your gut—but with the qualification that one should not overthink their decision."[68]

This study helps us understand that listening to your gut while making a difficult decision is critical. If you simply try to rationalize it, you'll end up making a poor decision.

But it takes a balanced approach. When getting all the details about the decision, using logic is important to study the problem. But when you move to making a decision, you need to think about your emotions and use your intuition. After all, it can more quickly reference all your past decisions and emotions to find a solid answer. Don't rely only on logic or you will overthink it.

Your marketing gut isn't just another source of data, it's one of the most powerful data tools on the market.

In the world of data-driven marketing, one of the better ways to optimize is through A/B testing. That's exactly what our gut does. It's the poster child for A/B testing. Our gut is how we learn and grow as humans. It's how we instantly optimize and choose the best option. And it probably has better data integrity than many business databases.

If we rely solely on data and reason, we undermine our greatest resource. Our guts are massive databases of experience. Remember, emotions are really just an instant transfer of a massive amount of data and logic. True, they aren't omniscient. They can get it wrong sometimes, and they have plenty of biases. That's why we have to train them day after day—it takes time to build up that database.

And that's why someone new to marketing won't have the same gut as an experienced marketer. We trust those with experience because they've already made hundreds of similar decisions and can access those experiences in a split-second of emotion.

But there's more to trusting our guts than simply past experiences. By understanding how we interpret emotions to make decisions, we can change the way we process decisions. We can tap into both emotional and logical ideas. We can become more intuitive thinkers.

Our gut instincts can be just as much about *how* we make decisions as it is about the past experiences that influence our decisions. Think of the way that many intuitive leaders, both past and present, have made decisions. They listened to all the options and then made a bold decision that often doesn't seem rational.

They aren't making a decision based on their conscious executive function. Rather, they tap into their feelings. They intuitively sense how they feel about a decision. They train their hard drive to respond quickly to the *process* of decisions rather than just the data of stored experiences.

They're looking for anomalies in the process and allowing their subconscious to find new solutions. It's the same creative process as coming up with a new emotional advertising idea.

On the flip side, data is just as important. You can't ignore it. Sure, it's emotionless. But it can be the catalyst to big ideas and disruption. You can't bully your gut into chasing an idea that isn't based on solid data. You'll end up with a creative idea that has no backbone.

Data-driven marketing leads to brilliant ideas. Data isn't the end of the journey. On its own, data isn't going to solve your business problems or change the world. But it will inspire big ideas.

As long as we have brains and emotions, our gut is the perfect way to make a decision. In fact, it's the only way to make a decision. It's the way we are wired.

What we've learned from neuroscience and behavioral economists is that both logic and emotions have strengths and weaknesses. And that a balanced approach is essential. We have to think about every choice and action, with both systems. Only then will we be able to overcome the shortcomings of logic and emotion.

The era of the gut isn't dead. But we shouldn't rely solely on our instinct. We need a balance of both. Gut and data. Emotion and logic.

But when I make a difficult decision, it feels logical.

This may seem opposite of what feels natural. Normally if you have a hard problem, you want to slow down and consciously work it out. But when you consider how the mind works, it's easier to see what's going on.

When we're slowing down and thinking hard, it's because we're trying to force our neurons and dopamine to act. But they don't know what to do, and we're stuck. If it's a new experience, where there isn't a past memory and our gut isn't telling us how to act, those neurons and chemicals don't know what to do. This is hard. There's no emotional grease. Without enough emotional juices to make a memory easy, we have to work a little harder for it.

Most of us have experienced this, but that doesn't mean it's a better way. It's actually quite inefficient. It uses up a lot of energy as our body is tense, pupils dilate, and we focus on the task. Slowing down and thinking logically about a problem doesn't always result in an answer. Often, we walk away because of the strain and our subconscious works on it overnight. This is how the brain tries to be more efficient, by allowing the subconscious to do the heavy lifting.

Another way we try to force a logical decision is by brute force. Perhaps the emotion is there and our brains are completely lit up, but our CEO or executive function wants to add some checks and balance to the decision. So we embrace a little micromanagement over our emotions to ensure that the decision feels logical. Even though we're really just ignoring all the data in the emotion. Then we make a forced decision and later end up regretting it.

We have to remember that emotions aren't unrestrained animals. Emotions are actually an enormous amount of past logic and rational thought. And we also need to remember that emotions are a positive feedback loop. Once we make a decision, if we get a good emotional response afterwards, we feel good about it, and then we act. We usually won't act if the decision "feels" wrong. This means that you can overthink and force a "bad" decision because you're trying to ignore your gut emotions.

Logic is emotion. And vice versa.

One insight that stuck with me from early in my career was a bit of advice from one of my first bosses named Darrell Smith. He was a founder and partner of the tech agency Dallin Smith White. When I first interviewed with him in 1995, he told me an interesting philosophy on strategy.

Smith was a classic account guy and strategist, but he believed in both results and creativity. To him, finding the strategic insight behind any product that would drive sales was really a creative act. In essence, creativity and strategy are really the same thing.

For example, when writing a creative brief and discovering the singular message that you should focus on, you were using your creative muscles. Or when you build a company vision statement or come up with a challenger brand strategy, it's really just another form of creativity.

His philosophy helped form my opinion that both creative agencies and results agencies were right. Both sides were really using the same process. We just called them different terms, but the type of thinking was the same.

By knowing how the brain works, we understand better how these two elements of marketing come together.

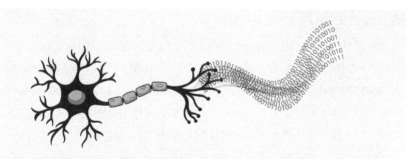

Emotions represent a massive amount
OF RATIONAL THOUGHT.

In terms of neuroscience, your marketing instinct is a series of past experiences, decisions, failures, and successes all rolled up into a nice emotional package. Instantly accessible and adaptable. Your gut experience is really a massive amount of past logic. Just like any memory.

So, here's a fascinating thought—*emotion is logic.*

Emotion represents a ton of rational thought. It's just expressed in a different way, through your fast system, rather than your slow system. But the data and experiences are the same things.

Like in our experiment of the fast system, the next time you feel an emotion, think of all the data that's communicated. Emotions are just a concentrated form of logic.

Just like creativity *is* strategy.

To the brain, both sides represent neurons firing in a pattern. It's just different flavors of the same action.

Which means it's not an either/or situation. The conflict is over. A balanced approach is really the only approach. Everyone is on the winning side.

Whole-brain marketing.

Now that we better understand how the mind uses emotion to function, it gives new insight into why marketing campaigns that use emotional ideas are more successful. For decades, advertising pros have known that emotional messaging pulls better. But they couldn't explain why. They just felt it in their guts.

However, now that we know how the brain ingests data, how it uses emotion to process it, and how emotion plays a pivotal role in decision making and creating memories, we have a universal answer that explains why emotional marketing is more effective.

This truth isn't based on a few unrelated case studies. It's not based on situational data. And it isn't formed from biased opinion. The role of emotion in how we pay attention and how we remember are physiological. It's built into the way each of us think and interact. It's part of us.

And this is a universal truth for all humans. There isn't a target audience like IT professionals who are different. Their brains work the same way all brains work. Which means we shouldn't make exceptions for certain audiences and only send them logical messages. Instead, the quest should be finding the right emotion for your specific audience. That's the whole point of creative ideas— emotional experiences that connect with an audience.

If we remove emotion from the equation, we are decreasing our chance for success. So the question becomes, why wouldn't you use strong emotions in your advertising and marketing?

Many logical thinkers have responded that emotional marketing is unnecessary. That it gets in the way of business. My guess is that response is simply based on tradition. They are following the prevailing thought that we are rational and that logical, linear thought is always right. Or perhaps we are so used to simply looking at the data that we dismiss emotions as something we can't measure. Therefore, they are extraneous.

As we've learned, that's just wrong. If marketing were purely a rational act, wouldn't we have already discovered that perfect marketing tactic? That ideal strategy that logically showed why your product is better. If that's the case, why don't customers choose the most logical product? The one with the better product benefits. Instead, they pick the brand they trust or connect with on a subconscious or emotional level.

How many ads do we love that are packed with great information? Do we instantly make a decision because we are presented with logical information?

Absolutely not.

In fact, more often the only decision many of us make is to ignore it completely.

Dismissing creative ideas as unnecessary is ignorant. What we should be asking as marketers isn't whether we should have an emotional message or a logical message, but instead we should be asking what emotion and data is right for each situation.

We should look deep into our customer data and find insights about our audience. Their triggers. We need to know what they care about, what fulfills their needs or what keeps them up at night. Then we should craft a message that rings true emotionally to those insights.

At the same time, we need to be careful to not over index on the creative side. Like many ads during the dot-com bubble of 2000. I saw many TV campaigns during that time that were just creative ideas without any substance or logic. They weren't tied back to the brand or the decision in any meaningful way. They were just crazy ideas designed to get attention, but nobody could remember who made them. This extreme of only emotion is also a bad strategy.

Yes, we need emotions to make decisions. So finding the right emotion is key to connecting with our customers when they are making decisions about our products. The more we can understand our customers and tap into their emotions, the better we can create brand experiences that last.

In two decades, I can't think of a logic-only ad campaign that I've worked on that has been so powerful that customers felt compelled to buy the product. But I have seen many emotional and creative campaigns that have compelled customers to action. They've become so loyal that they want to share the story with others so that they can feel it, too. We keep acting like being a consumer is a rational decision, when it's an emotional one.

Some may argue that there are deeper-funnel experiences where the consumer already has a relationship with the brand and these transactional messages can be direct and straightforward.

I'll discuss this topic in a later chapter on brand tone, but the quick answer is that we should still balance logic and emotion in every communication. Even a transactional email. Sure, the balance may be more logic than emotion. We shouldn't have a highly emotional headline at every level. But we should still have an approachable tone or keep a bit of humanity in the message.

Part of the art of being a great marketer is knowing the right balance of emotion to logic in every situation. You have to decide how much calculator to use versus tapping into the computing power of the whole laptop.

It's this balanced approach that's the best strategy. Not all logic. Not all emotion. But something that engages both systems at every level. Where you light up the whole brain of your customer as much as possible. We need whole-brain marketing.

Which means it's no longer about creativity versus results. With whole-brain marketing, it's about creativity *and* results. Branding *and* direct marketing. Art *and* science.

Logic and emotion can live hand in hand. Heart and mind. We are both rational and emotional when the whole brain is working.

ACT III—

PUTTING IT ALL INTO PRACTICE

Chapter 10

INSIGHT INTO THE STANDARD MARKETING PITCH

As we explore whole-brain marketing and how we make deci-sions, it helps to have a sense of what marketing experts have been pitching over the past decade. At least how they have con-nected creative ideas with improving the bottom line.

These are the same thoughts I shared with Russell when he asked if our billboard ideas would work. As marketers, we experi-ence enough campaigns over the years and we start to understand how messages and audiences are connected. We get a sense for certain messages that will resonate, and we recognize those that won't. This is the marketing gut.

After we go through the basic pitch, we'll look at it again with a neuroscience perspective. That way, we aren't just basing it on experience, but showing how science explains it all.

Here's the basic pitch that I've experienced from a number of agencies, marketing departments, and creative boutiques.

We'll go through this quickly so you get the backstory on how this has been presented. It starts by describing all the millions of messages that bombard consumers every day. The sheer number of media choices given to consumers is enormous, with endless photos, ads, videos, texts, emails, billboards, and apps. People's brains should be overloaded before they finish breakfast. Except they've learned to block most of them.

1. Get noticed
2. Be engaging = stickiness
3. Be believed
4. Be remembered = brand preference
5. Loyalty

And the only way to break through all that clutter and get noticed is with an emotional idea. It can be expressed in a few words, in an image, in a story—as long as it is told in a way that pulls on an emotion with the audience. That emotion can be comedy, inspiration, sorrow, or appreciation. The level of stand-out power depends on the amount of emotion. Something that is really emotionally charged will have more impact than something with a flutter of emotion.

The reason you need an emotional idea is because it causes more participation from the audience. Emotions draw people into the conversation. They react to the image or story. When they feel an emotion, they feel more connected. When we create ideas that require a little bit of participation from the audience, this creates an experience. Noticing an ad is one thing. Experiencing it is so much better.

We call this experience with your brand being "sticky." Which means the idea lasts longer in their mind. When your audience participates in the experience, their engagement level goes up. The more they are engaged, the stickier the experience becomes. Creative ideas create these moments of deeper engagement.

This sticky factor is important to the success of a piece of communication because it gives it a greater chance of being liked. When consumers have a positive experience and feel engaged, they create positive memories of the experience. These positive experiences over time create brand preference, which is another way of saying your customers like your brand.

Finally, people who have positive experiences with a brand become more loyal and are willing to pay more for that experience again. Brands are built on positive feelings over many experiences. And if you can consistently keep the positive experiences coming, your customers will remain loyal to your brand.

In short, a creative idea creates a chain reaction that eventually turns into brand loyalty. Here's a quick summary:

A creative idea **stands out** with an **emotional charge** that leads to audience **participation** that leads to greater **stickiness** that creates a **positive experience** that leads to greater **likability** that leads to repeat purchase and finally **brand loyalty**.

That's the basic pitch behind the value of a creative idea. At least, these are the reasons marketing experts have used over the years to explain why creative ideas work better.

If you break it down, these steps in the process are basically the secret sauce behind a large part of advertising agency proprietary approaches. Check several agency websites and you'll find a short narrative that explains their unique approach. They just all focus their narrative on a different part of this basic pitch.

Perhaps it's, "We create engagement." Or, "We are storytellers." Another may claim, "We create culture." Many others simply state that they put your customer at the center, or they're influencers, or builders of loyalty. Really what all these companies are claiming is that they understand this basic process. They know how to connect with people through emotional experiences and create a lasting connection.

Now, let's go through each step of that same pitch, not based on gut experience, but based on the neuroscience I've presented in this book. We'll look at it from a logical perspective on how the brain works and explain all these marketing buzzwords with science.

Getting noticed, with neuroscience.

As consumers, we're bombarded with millions of messages every day. Just scanning one page of search results or a long list of news stories can overwhelm the conscious mind. To avoid decision paralysis, our brains use a trick that's been hardwired into our system for ages. We use our subconscious skills of *anomaly detection*.

Our fast system is the first to kick in. It can quickly process more data than our slow logical system. It's the first to know if the idea is novel such as an anomaly or just another repeated view of our surroundings.

As our eyes or other senses flood our brains with an endless stream of inputs and stimulus, our fast brain efficiently processes and anticipates all that data, and only retains the most interesting data points. The rest are passed over in order to retain storage space. This isn't hard. Our brains do this every second of life, whether we're looking at media or not.

When we hear the stories of how we are being inundated with thousands of marketing messages, this is old news to our brains. This is the part of the pitch that we've had wrong over the years. The ever-increasing number of messages isn't the problem. Bring it. Our subconscious can handle millions of data points flooding in.

We've heard of studies where we only have five seconds to get a consumer's attention, or ten seconds on a web page, or that we give an average of seven eye flicks to each message. Whether that real number is a second or two-tenths of a second, it doesn't matter. A blink is plenty of time for our subconscious minds to decide if there is an anomaly and let us know if it's worth our time to take notice.

I want to pause on this point for emphasis. In the digital economy, we are constantly being told that our content needs to be bite-sized. Short. Fast. But marketers are getting this all wrong. The length or size doesn't matter. All that matters is if there is an anomaly. Something new or different. Something expressed with an unexpected emotion. I could create a small chunk of content that just gets ignored because it isn't an anomaly.

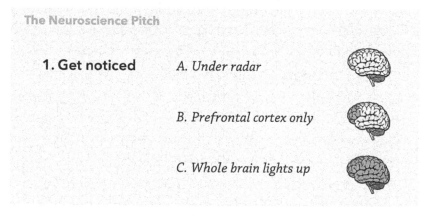

The Neuroscience Pitch

1. Get noticed   *A. Under radar*

B. Prefrontal cortex only

C. Whole brain lights up

When you send a message out to consumers in hopes that they will see it, three possible actions will happen.

First, and this is the worst-case scenario, your message goes completely under their radar. It's ignored. Your customers see the message, and in a split second, their brains reject the idea. It's not an anomaly. It's not worth giving any attention. It becomes wallpaper and they pass it by.

The second option is that the message registers, but only a small part of their brain lights up. This would be a classic straightforward message. Just the facts. In this example, your conscious brain slows down and absorbs the information. Remember, with straight-up logic, our memory can only handle a few variables. And it takes a lot of energy to analyze the data when our slow system is in charge. Which means the chances of our brains spending the minimal amount of energy on the idea is real. In this slow state, we try to hurry up and move along, focusing on other things.

Or perhaps your message remains in the subconscious only. It isn't a big anomaly, so it dabbles around for a bit and then is logged away. It thinks about the information for a short time, but then moves on. Perhaps it isn't a big enough deal to notify your executive function. Or if it does, there's no emotion, so your brain isn't flooded with neurochemicals. Perhaps the prefrontal cortex gives it a little attention, processes that data point, and then it's over. Your message got through, but it didn't make a grand entrance.

This is often the fate of a straightforward, logical idea. It has no emotion, so it only lights up a small part of the brain. Engagement is limited. And it probably doesn't move on to the next phase of locking in a memory. It's a flash in the slow-system pan. This is not a response you want from a prospective customer.

The third option is more dramatic. Your idea is noticed because it's a full-fledged anomaly. It's an emotional idea, and the brain instantly triggers a burst of neurochemicals. The emotion pulls from a variety of experiences as your subconscious quickly relates the new emotion to the past. Think of our exercise when you read the list of brand names and images and you were instantly filled with past thoughts and emotions. The experience was instantaneous. Much faster than seven eye flicks or even a second.

All of this happens lightning fast as your subconscious raises the flag and alerts your CEO. Your brain is flooded with emotion, causing multiple areas to light up. And when you make a decision to get engaged, your brain continues to be flooded with emotion and electricity. In short, your whole brain is alive and alert.

The difference between these last two options is striking. It's like standing in the shadows or being on center stage under the flood lights. When a burst of emotion is present in the brain, your message is on fire.

So really, the story of this first step isn't so much that we are flooded with too many messages and we need to stand out from the crowd. It's that your message needs to be emotional so that your message lights up your customer's entire brain. *The key to making an idea get noticed is emotion.* Not just information.

When we look at getting noticed from a neuroscience perspective, the key ingredient is emotional juice. When you present an idea to your audience, you want their brain to fire up like crazy. You need that emotional catalyst. You don't want to play it safe and just send a logical fact or you risk an efficient brain that will file away your idea too quickly. Sure, it may get through, but it won't get any fanfare.

Rather, you want that customer to wake up and instantly pay attention. This requires an anomaly and a flood of emotion. Which is another way of describing a standout creative idea.

A creative and emotional idea will break through, not because your brain does a SWAT analysis to break through all the other competing messages. But because the emotional idea immediately shoves out the competition and gets the brain to spend its energy on your message.

Engaging ideas that stick.

Let's assume your message lit up the whole brain and caught your target's attention. The next phase of the basic pitch is about engagement that leads to sticky experiences.

From a neuroscience perspective, this next step is a continuation from the first. When the brain is full of electricity and emotion, it's fully engaged. A brain that has only a few parts that are lit up isn't really engaged. It still has plenty of untapped power that is busy humming away on other data.

Remember how Dr. Simon taught that our brains don't retain everything. Maybe 10 percent of all input data.[69] Our subconscious sifts through all the messages and only keeps what's new or necessary. We have to let some things drop in order to stay efficient with the little energy we have. So if a thought or decision doesn't spike the brain with neurochemicals, then it's chances of survival and engagement are slim.

The argument of just getting to the product benefits or facts of the message first limits your engagement. These facts may live in short-term logic land for a brief visit, but then they move on and are lost in a sea of data.

If you want your ideas to engage people, you need to light up as much of their brain as possible. You want your left and right side engaged—both the forest and the trees. You want a flood of emotion. You want more neurochemicals released. You want that noodle on fire. Stickiness and engagement require emotions.

In the book *Made to Stick*, Chip and Dan Heath explore why some ideas stick and others don't.

For more than a decade, Chip and Dan researched the idea of stickiness. They studied with great teachers and entrepreneurs. They spent hundreds of hours collecting and analyzing sticky ideas, stories, and theories. The results were compiled and used for both Dan's startup company Thinkwell and with Chip's students at Stanford University.

What they discovered is that sticky ideas share common characteristics. And they aren't what most of us would expect.

"Given the importance of making ideas stick, it's surprising how little attention is paid to the subject. When we get advice on communicating, it often concerns our delivery: "Stand up straight, make eye contact, use appropriate hand gestures. Practice, practice, practice (but don't sound canned)." Sometimes we get advice about structure: "Tell 'em what you're going to tell 'em. Tell 'em, then tell 'em what you told 'em." Or "Start by getting their attention—

tell a joke or a story." Another genre concerns knowing your audience: "Know what your listeners care about, so you can tailor your communication to them." And finally, there's the most common refrain in the realm of communication advice: Use repetition, repetition, repetition."[70]

After digging into what makes ideas sticky, they discovered that many of these standard approaches are no longer valid. For example, a sticky idea doesn't need to be repeated ten times. Naturally sticky ideas are locked in on the first time they are heard.

Instead, they found six principles that help make ideas sticky. These six are *simple, unexpected, concrete, credible, emotional,* and *stories.*

Simple is all about focus. One message is better than ten. Don't boil the ocean. Find the core idea and stick to it.

Unexpected is about violating expectations. Being counterintuitive. Creating interest and curiosity. Make your idea an anomaly.

Concrete is about being clear. (Not just about the facts.) According to the Heaths, "Explain our ideas in terms of human actions, in terms of sensory information." Use concrete images and words so that your idea means the same to everyone.

Credible requires authority. Most go instantly for statistics or hard numbers, but that's the wrong approach. Sticky ideas let people test the idea for themselves. It's like self-initiated authority. They have to believe it for themselves.

Emotional is about making people feel something. Find the right emotion for the situation, not just the obvious one. We care about the human condition, not abstract ideas.

Stories get people to act. When we hear stories, we are allowed to live the experience without having to perform it ourselves. We create emotional memories that we can quickly reference when a new situation presents itself.

And the one factor they noticed that prevents us from creating sticky ideas is the curse of knowledge. Knowing too much makes us focus on unimportant data. We lose sight of a simple and unexpected idea and try to cram in all the product benefits.

These six principles align perfectly with creative and emotional ideas. They also line up with the standard marketing pitch: Capture their attention (unexpected) in a way that they understand it (concrete) and therefore believe it (credible), which means they will care (emotional) and finally take action (story).

The Neuroscience Pitch

1. Get noticed
2. Sticky

A. *We don't retain everything*

B. *More brain activity, more chance to lock in*

C. *More emotions, more neurons are trained*

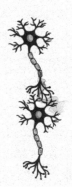

Bringing this idea of being sticky back to neuroscience, these principles also line up with our story so far. Emotional ideas are simple and unexpected (we've been calling them an anomalies). Concrete ideas are human, which means they bring up old images and words from your subconscious that are relatable and emotional. Credible ideas are believable because you've compared them through emotion with existing memories and you feel good about them. And finally, stories are a common way that we express feelings about the human condition.

You'll notice that terms such as statistics, facts, and logic weren't on the list of sticky principles. Yet when many marketers aren't hitting their numbers, the kneejerk reaction is to play it straight and avoid any emotion at all.

But as we've discussed, all logic without emotion won't work. It's wallpaper. Like corporate jargon and marketing speak. These aren't the types of ideas that stick. No matter how much we think that they will resonate with our target audience. They don't light up the whole brain. Again, logic is slow and short term. If you want to cause more neurons to fire and more neurochemicals to prepare more synapses for locking in a long-term memory, you need emotional and creative ideas in the mix.

You need a balanced approach. Emotions are essential to engagement. If you want to be sticky, logic alone doesn't cut it.

Ideas that are liked are remembered.

Now that the brain is flowing with emotional juice, the next part of the pitch is about whether we retain that idea or reject it. What will improve our chances of believing the message and remembering it?

Let's consider two options. The first is an idea that doesn't cause the brain to be flooded with emotion. In this instance, the process of laying down a memory trace is more difficult. There aren't as many neurochemicals to make the memory strong. Which means the repeating pattern between neurons that makes the memory isn't primed with emotion. The result could be a weak memory trace that could fade, or worse yet, no memory is made at all. We simply think about it for a moment in our short-term memory and then it's gone.

The second option is that the idea really pulls on our emotions. Our brains are flowing with electricity and emotions and neurochemicals. With all of these elements present, the chances of locking in a strong memory pattern are increased. The communication between neurons is constant and instantaneous. All this helps us lay down a strong memory trace and it helps increase the chances that we will more easily recall this memory. This is the holy grail of marketing—a message that is not only believed, but remembered.

And one of the little neurochemicals that makes all this emotion possible is dopamine. It's the grease that keeps the gears of memory making moving. But it also plays a major role in rewarding our behavior. The release of dopamine in our brains is the source of our happiness. Most addictive drugs release more dopamine, which is why users feel such a great high. And it's also an essential ingredient for ideas that are remembered by consumers.

Actually, to put it more boldly, it's one of the most important factors in determining if an idea will connect with your audience.

Another way of saying it is when we have more dopamine present, the more we like the message. And according to Eric Du Plessis, the biggest factor that influences whether your advertisement or content is remembered is centered on the idea of being liked.

In his book *The Advertised Mind*, Du Plessis describes the connection between emotions and message performance.

"It is the emotional properties of those memories that determine whether we pay attention or not, and how much attention we pay. The more intense the emotional charge of the associated memories, the more attention we pay. If the charge is positive, it is likely we will feel attracted to what is happening. If it is negative, we will feel repelled.

"This is one reason why advertising that creates a positive emotional response performs better than that which does not—a fact repeatedly borne out by tracking studies the world over."[71]

Du Plessis explains his quest that spanned several decades in trying to determine which factors make the biggest difference in successful advertising messages. As the owner of a media research company, he conducted thousands of tests on advertising messages to figure out which elements were most effective. With a large database of commercials and advertisements, he and many others were able to test and rate effectiveness across a wide spectrum that included media length, channels, and other criteria.

In addition to his research, the American Advertising Research Foundation also found the same results in their major study called the Copy Research Validation Project.

In these and other studies done by media researchers, there was one factor that made the biggest difference by a long shot. It wasn't the length of a video. It wasn't the number of times we repeated the message. It wasn't the type of media.

That single most important factor was likeability.

The Neuroscience Pitch

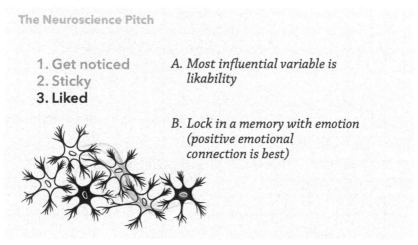

1. Get noticed
2. Sticky
3. **Liked**

A. *Most influential variable is likability*

B. *Lock in a memory with emotion (positive emotional connection is best)*

According to Du Plessis, "The objective of this major study (The American Advertising research foundation), managed by Russ Haley and undertaken by a body that had no axe to grind, was to find out which copy-testing research question was the most predictive of a commercial's actual selling ability. It measured advertisements on all the commonly used copy-testing measures, and found that the simple question, 'How much do you like the advertisement?' was the best predictor.

"The conclusion researchers reached was that more than 40 percent of the variation in effectiveness was explained simply by ad-liking scores. If the advertisement is liked, then its ability to create awareness doubles."[72]

For media researchers who have no stake in the message, that's a fascinating conclusion. Certainly, they would hope that longer commercials or more media would be ideal. And yet today, with the rise of digital, we continue to test things such as video length and other data points about the delivery of the message. What we should be focused on is how to create messages that consumers actually like.

Du Plessis continued to analyze his research to discover how you get people to like your advertisements. He came up with a few suggestions.

"Ad-liking is caused by things like humor, characters, aspirational situations, and news that is relevant to the reader."

His longer list of likable messages includes topics such as entertainment, empathy, and familiarity. And he cautions us to avoid the opposite of liking, with messages that hit negative emotions including confusion and alienation.

The core idea of his research is this—messages that work are those that are liked.

Du Plessis summarized the results, "The most important building block of both recognition and attribution is whether people liked the advertisement. In fact, 80 percent of the variation in recognition is determined by ad-liking, and 51 percent of the variation in attribution is explained by ad-liking."

"Every advertiser should try to make advertising that consumers like, for a very simple reason: it acts as a multiplier of the effectiveness of the media budget."

His research and advice live in perfect alignment with our understanding of neuroscience. When our brains are flooded with emotional dopamine, we like the ad and we like the brand. Which in turn helps us more easily retain memories about those positive experiences.

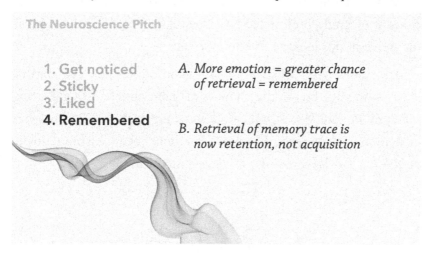

The Neuroscience Pitch

1. Get noticed
2. Sticky
3. Liked
4. Remembered

A. *More emotion = greater chance of retrieval = remembered*

B. *Retrieval of memory trace is now retention, not acquisition*

Inside the brain, we have just processed a positive experience. A memory track has been burned into the neurons and is locked in place with a corresponding emotion. That emotion is now part of your subconscious database. Whenever that memory is retrieved or if the brain cross references new experiences against that memory, a lightning fast feeling will be released. The release of dopamine as part of that positive memory will remind you that you like that brand.

Positive experiences are core to us liking, believing, and remembering messages. As marketers and idea creators, we really need to absorb this concept. The most important factor for retention is if the idea is liked.

Businesses that prioritize likable experiences will have an edge on the competition. It's that simple.

When you're faced with picking an idea to use in an upcoming marketing campaign, don't let yourself rationalize away with logic and choose the safe message. Be bold and go with something you actually like. Because if that message is liked, it multiplies your chances of being believed and remembered.

Brand preference becomes loyalty.

Moving along to the final step in the basic pitch, we reach the concept of brand preference and eventually brand loyalty. This is the step that ties ideas to the bottom line.

The more your customers are exposed to positive experiences with your brand, the chances of them preferring your brand increase. In addition, if you can become a preferred brand by your customers, you increase the chances of them becoming brand loyal. And often loyalty turns into increased income.

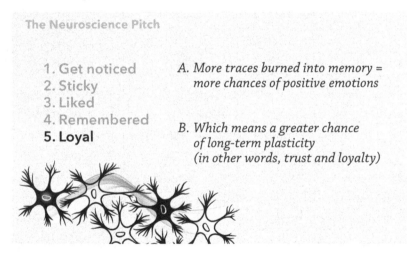

The Neuroscience Pitch

1. Get noticed
2. Sticky
3. Liked
4. Remembered
5. Loyal

A. *More traces burned into memory =
more chances of positive emotions*

B. *Which means a greater chance
of long-term plasticity
(in other words, trust and loyalty)*

These last steps aren't really something that many argue about. Most of us want loyal customers. We're usually just haggling over how to get them.

So, to finish off the neuroscience journey on the creative pitch, let's discuss what happens in the brain after we lay down a memory track. Hopefully the memory trace is strong, meaning the pattern was repeated with a strong emotion and it's easy for us to recall.

If so, whenever we have another experience with that brand, our subconscious database quickly scans the data and releases a hit of dopamine, reminding us that our memory of this brand was a positive experience.

As long as the brand holds true to the experience and continues to delight the customer, we increase the chances of reinforcing the memory with another positive emotional response. This acts as a positive loop response, with each new experience reinforcing the old experiences. We not only build up the original experience and make that memory trace stronger, but we also create new memories and experiences that are associated with the brand.

All of these additional exposures to positive experiences create more powerful emotions surrounding the brand.

At this point in the customer journey, you have hopefully reached brand preference. The only caution here is to continue to surprise and delight the customer in order to keep the memories strong. Don't screw things up. If you prioritize engaging customer experiences, you can eventually create a strong enough database of good emotions that your customer will become loyal.

Once your customers are already engaged and have positive experiences, there is ample opportunity for a brand to offer deeper messaging that may be more logical than emotional. These experiences will help reinforce exposures to the positive brand feelings. They may not be ideas that inherently create new emotions, and they may only light up the logical areas of the brain. But they will extend the positive goodwill and can lay down additional knowledge tracks that build up the greater whole.

On the flip side, without additional exposure or positive reminders, even strong memories can fade. Or a negative experience could sully the whole brand database. The takeaway is that brands need to constantly offer positive emotional experiences to keep the memories strong and push customers toward loyalty.

The entire customer journey needs emotion.

Now that we've reviewed the entire pitch through the lens of neuroscience, how does this help us in real world marketing situations? Most likely, we aren't going to keep a long checklist or fMRI machine handy so we can run down the list of what's happening in the brain to be more effective.

The take away from this exercise is understanding how important emotional ideas are in the entire customer journey. They aren't just important in the getting attention phase.

Logic is important too, but we rarely have an issue of not having enough data. The problem in business today is giving emotion an equal opportunity.

The right balance of emotional and rational ideas is important at every step of the journey. In the discovery phase, emotions are critical in pushing out other thoughts and putting your idea on center stage so you can tell your data and story. During the explore phase, emotions play a key role in comparing the data of past experiences to the memory database and they help facilitate the ideal conditions for the establishment of new memories. And finally, at the evaluate phase, when a customer is ready for more information on whether the product is the right solution, emotions still help maintain brand recognition, preference, and eventually loyalty. The balance may change through the journey, but never suppose that emotions aren't necessary at every step.

Creative and emotional ideas are the best option to get noticed quickly. They make your ideas stickier. They're more believable. They're more engaging. They're more likable. They help facilitate stronger memories. And they help maintain brand preference and loyalty.

This whole process of how we notice ideas, engage with ideas, believe ideas, and eventually remember ideas is all guided by emotion. This whole narrative isn't about the process being ruled by rational thought or logic. Our rational brain plays a role, but it isn't the main character. Emotion is at the center.

In a fast-paced industry, our fast, emotional system is the one that initially leads the charge on how we will engage with marketing ideas. And it's the common denominator throughout the entire customer journey.

So when it comes down to Russell's big question at the opening of this book, whether a creative idea or a direct statement will work better, the answer is a no brainer.

Chapter 11

BRAND VOICE GETS A TUNE-UP

Before the meeting about our new website even starts, Jason is fuming mad. He sits down at the conference room table and folds his arms, glaring at me as his jaw flexes. He skips the pleasantries and gets to the point.

"Why do we always have to put that marketing fluff into the headline? We're talking to an IT director. They don't care about this crap. They need information. Why don't we just give it to them. They are data heads. They want it direct and straightforward. Period."

I thought that the headline was creative and effective. But at this point, I have two choices. Fight for my point of view. Or find common ground.

I've experienced countless meetings like this one with Jason. Two sides fighting for different expressions of the brand. One creative. One direct and straightforward. Early in my career as a creative writer, I was taught by my creative directors to always fight for your ideas. Push back on the product marketers. The strategists. The client. The only way a creative idea would survive is if you never gave up.

While I have as much tenacity as the next person, I never believed that marketing should be a warzone. And because I appreciate both sides, the creative and strategic aspects of marketing, I never felt good about digging in my heels and being a jerk about the process of idea creation.

I also knew that there had to be a way to take the focus off of the two warring sides and find a solution that brought the best of strategy and creativity together. In marketing, creativity and strategy can live in harmony.

Certainly there is the challenge of getting buy-in from both sides. If you suggest compromise to the creative department, they consider you a sellout hack. If you suggest compromise to the strategists and marketing managers, they treat you as a less-educated marketer who doesn't understand metrics.

Fortunately, after years of experience, and thanks to dozens of books and studies, I found a solution that has worked remarkably well.

Voice versus tone.

Before we discuss my solution, we must first understand what a brand's voice and tone really mean. Because so many people get it completely wrong.

Perhaps you've heard or read the term "tone of voice." Many use this term as a catch-all for a brand's personality. I usually hear something like, "Our brand's tone of voice is all about being intelligent and professional." Or, "It's our brand's tone of voice guidelines."

Right now, I'm experiencing the equivalent of fingernails on a chalkboard. Let me break down why statements like this are just wrong.

The *voice* of a brand is the character. The personality. A summary of values. It should never change.

The *tone* of a brand is the mood that the personality expresses at a specific moment in time. It changes constantly, just like our moods change.

The tone and voice are not the same thing for a brand. They are two distinct elements.

The voice is who we are. Our character may have depth, flaws, and strengths—but it represents what we stand for. People are attracted to strong brands because they represent something that they care about. We are not a chameleon and our voice should be consistent. If your brand is like an academic professor, intelligent and logical, you should never use a voice that is flip or full of slang, like a hipster. It would be off brand.

But the tone can change. Because we are human, we have mood swings. Sometimes we are happy. Sometimes somber. We talk to others with different moods based on the topic or situation.

Hopefully this distinction explains why you shouldn't use the term "tone of voice" incorrectly. It doesn't mean the whole brand personality. That's the voice. We describe the voice with terms that describe a person. Like professional, smart, and environmentally conscious.

If we are really talking about the tone *of* voice, we should be referencing a specific expression of the brand voice in a specific moment of time. We're talking about just the tone. Like a headline with a tone that's approachable. Copy with a tone that's caring and understanding.

We should refer to the brand voice and tone as separate elements in our marketing plans. Because a good brand should use both.

While it sounds like I'm on a soapbox, this distinction is the linchpin for finding common ground. A brand can have a consistent voice but still express different tones based on the situation. There can be times when the brand voice is emotional and engaging, and times when the brand voice is direct and to the point. We don't have to battle over it, we just need to know the appropriate time to express the various moments of tone.

Here's how we turned that into a real-world application of brain science and marketing philosophy.

The tone hierarchy.

Consider a traditional marketing funnel as it relates to messaging, not media or other factors. At the top of the funnel, you have messages that are intended to engage with the audience. As you travel down the funnel, you introduce deeper information about the product until you reach the moment of a sale.

In marketing, we can't give all messages equal importance in a brand experience. You need to prioritize them. Start with a key message that will resonate. Then add in more points as the customer continues to engage with you. This is the basic truth of any good messaging brief.

At some point, I realized that this same pattern of messaging can be used with the brand tone. Just as different messages are appropriate at different moments along a customer journey, the brand tone is no different.

On top of that, when you overlay major lessons learned in neuromarketing, you get a similar pattern — such as the fact that our fast, emotional systems engage with brand experiences first, and our slow, logical systems kick in later.

Mixing these three truths of marketing, we find common ground.

I call it the tone hierarchy, and it can help guide the tone you use for a variety of marketing situations.

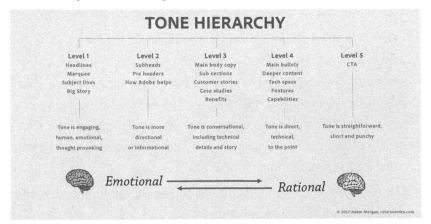

TONE HIERARCHY

Level 1	Level 2	Level 3	Level 4	Level 5
Headlines	Subheads	Main body copy	Main bullets	CTA
Marquee	Pre headers	Sub sections	Deeper content	
Subject lines	How Adobe helps	Customer stories	Tech specs	
Big Story		Case studies	Features	
		Benefits	Capabilities	
Tone is engaging, human, emotional, thought provoking	Tone is more directional or informational	Tone is conversational, including technical details and story	Tone is direct, technical, to the point	Tone is straightforward, short and punchy

Emotional ⟶ ⟵ Rational

© 2017 Adam Morgan, returnonidea.com

For example, we know that our subconscious brain is faster than our logical brain. And that using a strong emotion at the introduction phase will help us stand out. But as you move through the messaging journey, you can't stay at that high emotional level. Sometimes you have to introduce more direct messages. The result of the tone hierarchy is creating that balance of both. You need the pacing of both styles in the messaging for it to sound natural and human.

There are times when a more emotional and creative message is critical. But there is also a time and a place for a more logical message. The result is that both sides win. We don't have to fight over having the entire message being direct or the entire message being creative. It's just a question of knowing the right moment to use the right tone.

In this tone hierarchy, we have five levels of messaging. Level one is the first priority of any piece of marketing material. This is the first message our audience reads. It could be a headline, a subhead, a subject line, whatever is designed to be read first. Think of this as the top of the funnel (this chart is like a funnel on its side, top of funnel on the left, bottom at the right). At level one, the tone should be more emotional, engaging, and thought provoking. We are trying to take advantage of that fast emotion in our subconscious brain. We need emotions to get the brain to fire up, and we want the audience to quickly engage with us.

As you get deeper into the messaging experience, into a level two or three, you begin to balance the tone between emotional ideas and logical ideas. The emotion is still present in the experience, but so are more directional and logical thoughts. The balance helps maximize the need for an emotional anomaly and product information. For example, at a level three, typical in the main body copy of an email or web page, the tone is more conversational, with more concrete details of the story or product benefits.

Email Example

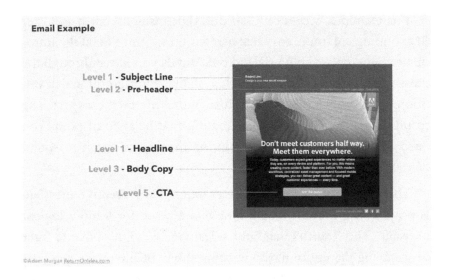

©Adam Morgan ReturnOnIdea.com

As you progress to the right of the funnel, the tone of the message continues to change. At a level-four message, the tone is more technical and straightforward. Here, the messaging includes elements such as bullet points, deeper product features, or technical capabilities. At this point in the customer journey, the message shouldn't be super creative and emotional. We already have the audience's attention. The brain is already lit up from the messaging in higher levels. Instead, this is our chance to communicate all those important facts that seal the deal.

And when you finally reach level five, or the bottom of the funnel, you're ready for a call to action. A call to action should be short and straightforward. No more emotional crap. We want to be very clear about what action we want our audience to take. This type of messaging is logical and direct.

All five levels aren't required for every ad or experience. With a billboard, you may only have time and space for level one and level five. With a website, you use all five levels. Simply match the levels of tone to the medium.

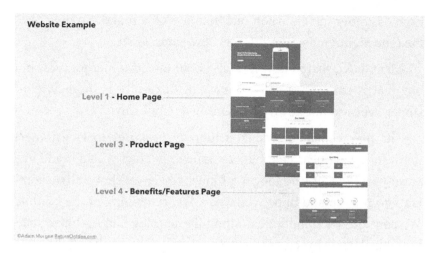

At the same time, within a lower-level web page, you can't eliminate all emotion. You still need a bit of humanity to keep the flow. Otherwise we end up with a first-generation web page from 1994 with only a list of bullets and links. Just find the right balance of levels, where maybe the headline is a level three with some conversational tone, and other parts of the page are more informational.

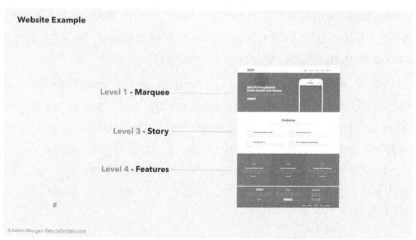

The right tone for every step.

To be fair, funnels are outdated. We know that customers today don't follow a linear path. There are dozens of unique paths that each customer travels when interacting with a brand. So how does the tone hierarchy work with this new paradigm?

Many have shared new models about the customer journey, but one that is simple yet offers plenty of flexibility is the new consumer decision journey by McKinsey & Company.[73]

The new consumer decision journey proposes that customers don't follow a linear path but continue to interact with a brand in a variety of ways. It's no longer a funnel where we shove all customers into the top and hope we have a few remaining at the bottom. We consider each individual along the journey and optimize their individual path by creating personal experiences that help them stay loyal.

To put it in simple terms, imagine that there are several steps along the brand journey. At any given time, a customer can move from one step forward or backward in the journey. As customers move, the next step can offer a variety of choices, so that the path isn't linear. But in order to market effectively, we just need to know where that individual is currently on the path and what choices are available. Will they choose to buy, move toward loyalty, move back a step, or choose a different product?

As we market, each step is as critical as the entire old-school funnel. Moving to a new step requires the right messages to get them on that step and to keep them there. Because unlike the traditional funnel model, customers can go back a step in the experience. Or they can take a side path. We have to engage them at multiple moments with emotional ideas to keep them connected to the brand.

Typically, branding and emotion are used heavily at the top of the marketing funnel. The thought is to grab an audience's attention at the beginning with a great emotional hook. Then as you journey down the funnel, you move to more logical thoughts and more information. Going back to the debate of branding versus direct marketing, emotions shouldn't be limited to one part of the process.

If we apply the lessons learned from Damasio, this makes sense. If the decision-making process requires emotions all the way to validation, we should make sure our communications retain a bit of emotion throughout the journey.

Every step of the journey requires a decision. Customers can either choose to accept one aspect of your marketing plan and move closer to becoming a brand advocate, or they can decide to move back along the journey away from a purchase.

At every moment of the customer journey, we are using both logic and emotion. It's easy to move back and forth on different steps, so we need the emotion as validation at every step to encourage the right decision.

When I compare that model to the tone hierarchy, I think of each of the five levels as a mini checklist for each step. With every experience, we have to use the various messaging levels to maintain the relationship.

For example, if you think of a single piece of communications as a step, you need the appropriate levels of tone. Take an individual email for example. To quickly get them engaged, we need a level-one headline that is creative and emotional. We also need some concrete data at some point in the experience to keep it sticky.

But if you look at the example of an entire website, the whole experience matches the customer chain model. Each page is a step along the journey. And each page may need a level-one emotional hook as well as the other levels as you progress through the experience. We don't have an emotional headline for the main homepage and then ignore emotion throughout the website. Because users can get bored and click away at any moment. Each page should be treated as an individual experience or step with the corresponding levels of tone.

However, we also need to look at the website as a whole, like one big step. So as you get deeper into the experience, you get more concrete data. For example, on a third-tier product page, you should have more straightforward messaging and product information than the homepage. But you still need a few emotional hits to keep the neurochemicals flowing and engagement high.

It's a big balance across the whole experience where we need to use the right emotion and logic to create a balanced experience every step of the journey.

Create your peace treaty.

This hierarchy may seem simple, but for many it has helped bridge the gap between creative and logical messages. Teams no longer have to fight about tone in an email or banner ad. We all know that the headline or top level is going to be emotional and creative. Otherwise it won't drive engagement. But the call to action shouldn't be a creative exercise. The CTA should be bold and direct.

For many logical thinkers, this hierarchy gives a logical structure to how we create marketing materials. They know that the facts aren't going to be ignored, they just have a time and a place. For the creative thinkers, it defines a clear sandbox where they can play with emotion without constant fear of ideas being killed.

Of course, you should create a custom tone hierarchy for your brand. You may have a brand voice that is more logical all the time, so your levels of emotion and logic may adjust. Or your brand voice is more playful or lives on the cutting edge. Then you may want more emotional tone throughout the experience.

By using our knowledge of brain science and how that affects the customer journey, this hierarchy helps us know the right moments to express the right tone in order to accomplish our marketing goals.

After that heated conversation with Jason, we were able to work out when and where the message should be direct and when it should appeal to our emotions. Even an IT director still uses the same process to make a decision. Their brains aren't unique. We no longer fight for one style or the other. With a better understanding of the brand tone, he realized we can use both approaches. We just need to match the right tone to the right message—while maintaining a consistent brand voice.

The brand voice never changes. But sometimes you have to be direct and logical. And sometimes you need a strong emotional idea.

With the right tone structure, you can have both.

Chapter 12

THE IDEAL LENGTH OF A HEADLINE

Throughout my career, I've had the constant debate with stakeholders about the most effective length of a headline. Most times people refer back to the concept of us only having three seconds to get the attention of the audience, which means we should only employ headlines that are only a few words, right? Because reading too many words would push you past that three second window and you will lose a customer.

I believe in the philosophy of restraint. It's the whole bed of nails analogy. If we have too many messages, rather than one, we won't penetrate the walls of resistance.

So I agree that an economy of words, like good poetry, can create a huge emotional response. But sometimes, I would come across a good headline and it may take more than four or five words to express an idea. But stakeholders would kill it because it looked too long.

Then I met Dan Greenberg, and I found an interesting answer to this question. Dan is a successful entrepreneur, and he built a company based on an interesting point of view about words and how they affect our engagement.

Words and the brain.

Greenberg's company, Sharethrough, is focused on native ads and how they engage more than traditional ads. But what makes his company unique from others in Silicon Valley is how he started the company. Before he started building a product or selling anything to customers, he first started with several studies in neuroscience.

He believed that native ads worked better. But it was a big bet and he wanted to make sure it was true. To Greenberg, product development and understanding the brain are inseparable. So one of the first employees he hired at Sharethrough was a neuroscientist.

When I asked him why this was so important, this was his explanation:

"The reason why we started our company in the first place is based on the notion that foreign objects can't be sustained as a business model forever. At the very beginning, we hired a full-time neuroscientist to prove our business model—that people will read native ads more than traditional ads. People are used to being interrupted with banner ads or video pre-roll. But we believed that when the ads fit in, then some interesting magic happens.

"In a typical experience, when you see an ad, your brain sees it as the other. Your brain sees that as a foreign object that doesn't deserve the same kind of cognitive activity that the core user experience should have. The hypothesis of our company is that if the ad fits in naturally to the user experience, then it will be processed the same way that the underlying content is processed. The brain will perceive the native ad with the same neural activity and process it as respectfully as the main content.

"When we focused on the neuroscience, we were able to prove our business model. And we discovered the kind of connections that people make with reading and how it's a really important mechanism for delivering meaning."[74]

Once he had proof that his business model was going to work, he didn't walk away from neuroscience. From startup to established company, he continues to place a high value on making sure his work meshes with how the brain works. Sharethrough is constantly conducting brain studies to ensure their business is going in the right direction.

And it's paid off. Sharethrough has found unknown insights that continue to help their business grow. Insights that can give us more context on the right length of a headline.

"One of the things that we discovered out of our neuroscience work that actually surprised us, is that there are a specific set of words that when these words hit your brain, you're more likely to stop and pay little bit more attention. And these aren't click bait, where we're trying to trick you into clicking, such as saying 'surprising results' or 'you'll never believe this.' It's not that, it's actually more about triggering your brain to stop and read the one word and then to read the next few words. We call this set of words 'context words' because they demand more context when you read them.

"These words trigger micro-attention, and once you have micro-attention, you earn a little millisecond of engagement as customers read your content, and then it's up to the rest of the headline to grab the rest of their brain's attention. It doesn't force attention, but it makes your brain say—OK, I'll give you a bit of micro attention. I'm with you now, so give me something interesting to read."

Greenberg's research isolated many keywords that have a higher probability to immediately stimulate your brain. Context words are packed with existing emotions. According to Greenberg, there are several categories of context words, such as connecting meaning with time, creating insight, relating with our physical space, and experiencing a feeling of motion.

Take the word *falling*, for example. It's a motion word, and when we read that word, our brains quickly look for more context because it's an action that brings up a lot of emotion. What's falling? Why is it falling? It's a word that connects with past emotional experiences and our brain instantly wants to fill in the next part to satisfy the action.

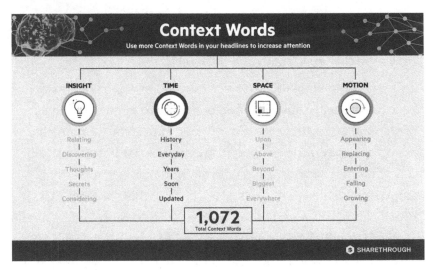

Sharethrough has categorized thousands of words that have a higher probability of containing built-in emotion. It may not be an absolute science because each of us has unique experiences with certain words. But it certainly gives us insight into searching for the right words for our messaging.

This search for meaning or context in language is the path that writers travel each time they stare at a blank page. And while seasoned writers have more experience in knowing which words evoke more meaning through trial and error, this type of research can help all marketers create better messaging.

Using words with more built-in emotion will drive better engagement. Context words can instantly disarm our defenses. This is important in initial engagement with a customer, as we need to not only inspire them, but we have to disable all of their internal filters in order to make an impression.

In terms of how this relates back to brain functionality, certain keywords quickly map back against our database of emotions and relay a positive association back to our conscious brain. These context words are like mini catalysts that add meaning and create more neural pathways.

Greenberg explains how context words are the secret to attention. "Reading stories is a much deeper and more effective way to impact the brain. Reading changes the brain by creating new associations or connections. And context words are the quickest way to access these deeper associations.

"If you can get someone to *read* content, you have a better chance at holding their attention. Because when your brains read it, you have a much stronger connection with the messaging than when we see an image on a page, when we're driving past a passive billboard, or even when leaning back and watching a video. Your brain is trained to constantly make connections between the words."

Our brains are a massive conglomeration of neural networks connecting billions of neurons. With everything we read and learn, our brains are constantly making new associations. As we try to persuade customers to believe in our brand, we are trying to make new associations and memories that connect positive emotions with the words and language we use every day.

Back to headline length.

Here's where context words help us understand the ideal length in a headline. From several studies about headlines, Greenberg claimed that longer headlines often result in higher engagement.

What Greenberg meant is that the key indicator of engagement had to do with the number of context words in the headline.

A longer sentence with several context words pulled more than a short sentence with just one or two. To be fair, the sentence can't just be a jumbled mix of context keywords. It must be a singular thought or coherent idea that creates an experience.

Your brain stalls for a microsecond on a context word, and if the next few words can offer more context, engagement increases. When your headline has several context words, your chances of holding attention also increases.

Think of this in terms of SEO. The more keywords that are found result in a higher position in the search results. And if we like the short description around that keyword, we click.

Digital has changed how we use keywords. Take digital resumes. In the past, a one-page resume was required so that the recruiter could process and understand your qualifications without be over-whelmed and lose interest. But with digital search algorithms for recruiting, a LinkedIn profile can be several pages long and packed with all the right keywords.

If you follow the paradigm of the past and create a LinkedIn profile that resembles a one-page resume, you are hurting your chances of being discovered. To increase your chances, you should use as many context words as possible, while maintaining a solid story of your experience. Because after the initial search, a real person is going to review your profile and a page of unconnected keywords will suddenly ruin your chances of recruitment.

This is how context words work with your subconscious. Like a recruiting algorithm, your subconscious can quickly scan headlines in search for emotionally charged words.

The length of the headline isn't as important as the content. If your brain finds a context word, it's more engaged and keeps reading. If it finds several of these context words tied together in a big idea, it will be more engaged.

But people scan headlines.

In a separate article by Kissmetrics, they found that the ideal length of a headline is all about scannability. Here is what they had to say about headline length.

"A headline you can read in a single glance obviously communicates its content more effectively than one you cannot. Usability research shows that people not only scan body copy, but headlines as well—and they tend to take in only the first and last 3 words. This suggests the perfect length for a headline is 6 words.

"Of course, that's seldom enough to tilt the specificity-meter into the red. And I have it on good authority that some of the highest-converting headlines on the web are as long as 30 words. As a rule, if it won't fit in a tweet it's too long. But let me suggest that rather than worrying about length you should **worry about making every word count.** Especially the first and last 3—and if that means using the passive voice, so be it."[75]

People certainly scan headlines, and their advice to make the first three and last three words count is fantastic. If we get all those context words into a nice scannable length of six words, all the better. But that's not always realistic when dealing with expressing a good idea.

When we combine the advice of scannability with the value of context words, you can see that engagement is more about the choice of words and content.

So the debate shouldn't be about length or the number of words in a headline. Or the amount of time it takes to read it, for that matter. There are times that a longer headline is the more effective answer because it has more emotionally charged words that are easy to scan.

Rather, we should change the conversation to what really matters. The conversation about headline length needs to transition and focus on the emotional content, including context words and ideas that engage audiences.

It's not always about how many words, but about using the right words.

This lesson from neuroscience can help in many areas of marketing. It seems like teams are constantly testing whether longer or shorter emails work better. Longer or shorter subject lines. Longer or shorter web pages and copy chunks.

The answer is more about the context and content than the length. If people are engaged, they will give you time. If your content is boring, they will move along, regardless of the length of copy.

Chapter 13

MAKING BETTER MARKETING DECISIONS

Imagine you're sitting at a large conference room table. A team of creatives are presenting a new campaign for your brand. The creative director stands up, full of excitement, and begins to explain a fresh perspective on your product.

As a cutting-edge marketer, you believe in the value of big ideas. But as you sit and listen to the creative pitch, you pause to think. How do you make sure you are objective and open minded? When presented with multiple campaigns, how can you be sure you pick the most effective idea? And you want to make sure that you don't let logic cloud your thinking. How do you actually make decisions on creative ideas that maintains the right balance of emotion and logic?

If you were in Russell's shoes, would you be able to not only make a judgment call on a creative idea, but could you also be confident enough to sell it up the organization?

Being a marketing decision maker is challenging. Your university degree taught you how to make marketing plans, orchestrate strategies, and balance a marketing budget. I'm not aware of many college courses on neuromarketing that focus on what goes on in the brain of the actual marketing decision maker.

In order to understand how to make better marketing decisions, first let's explore how creative people come up with new ideas in the first place. The parallel is enlightening.

The creative decision-making process.

Every Friday morning, a community of writers at Adobe meet for an hour-long video conference call. The purpose of these writer's workshops is to better understand the creative process and to learn how to apply it in our work. Best practices are shared. New campaigns are reviewed. And the entire group walks away inspired for the next week.

Recently, one of the writers, Rebecca Stately, shared a presentation about the unique processes that creative people use to come up with fresh ideas. She interviewed a handful of people with diverse jobs and backgrounds. A photographer from New York. A playwright from Chicago. A writer from Silicon Valley. And a painter from Boston.

Each individual had a very personal and unique process for coming up with creative ideas. One began the process by visiting a coffee shop first thing in the morning and watching people welcome the day. Another read comic books, then took a nap, and finally put on loud music while he cranked out new ideas. A third would visit art galleries, doodle in a blank notebook, go to therapy for a few hours every week, and eventually sit down to paint beautiful art. And finally, the fourth would read and read seminal works by other authors, visit with his shaman, and then binge write, sometimes for months at a time.

Certainly, anyone you ask who creates original content will have an individual process. Mine involves constantly sitting in different chairs. (That's right, inspiration is all about the right amount of rump cushioning.) But there are some common steps that most of us follow.

The creative process

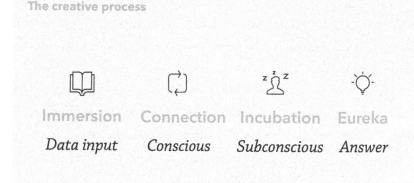

Immersion   Connection   Incubation   Eureka
Data input   *Conscious*   *Subconscious*   *Answer*

The first step is immersion. This is the phase where you soak in as much information as possible on the topic. Read and watch related content, books, and video. Fill the well with more knowledge on the topic than you will ever use. I call it building up your supply of idea fodder. This is all about data collection.

The second phase is raw idea generation. Armed with all that fodder, you start to make new connections and combine data in interesting ways. Because new ideas are most often simply a new connection of disparate elements. It's important to get past all the low hanging fruit to find original ideas. Chances are, you may get lucky in this phase, but more often you come up with derivative ideas. From a brain perspective, this is you trying to logically think it through and make new connections. It's the slow part of the process, but necessary.

Next is the incubation phase. Here's where you completely walk away from the project. Sleep on it overnight. Take a long walk. Go watch a movie. Distract yourself, but make sure you're in a comfortable environment. This gives your subconscious brain, or your fast system, a chance to process all the data and create more connections.

Even though it seems like this step is a waste of time, every creative person will tell you that it's essential in finding that eureka moment. What we don't realize is that constant analysis and cross referencing is still going on in our brains under the hood. Our subconscious brain is more powerful and can handle more data processing than our logical frontal lobe. You may be letting go of conscious control, but your brain is still working on it.

For this step, it's essential that you are in a relaxed state. That's why relaxing in bed or a hot shower are often the catalyst moments for a big idea. Your fast, subconscious system needs a chance to focus on the problem and you need to be willing to listen when it finds an answer.

After incubation, once we start thinking about the project, suddenly the ideas come faster. All the subconscious thinking has ordered the data. Now when we think about it, we can more easily make associations and new connections—and hopefully get that big hit of inspiration where everything comes together. We discover the answer.

For those who have trained their brain with this workflow, with practice, the ideas come faster. I can certainly confirm that the process took me much more time and effort at the beginning of my career. Today I can rip through this process in a more limited amount of time.

How this helps non-creative folks.

What does the creative process have to do with making marketing decisions? I would submit that the same process that's used to create an idea is just as valid when judging the same idea.

That's right, if marketers use the creative process while making *decisions* about creative ideas, they'll have a better chance at success.

Think of it as the process for intuitive thinking. This is the type of thinking that embraces both your logical and emotional brain. More often, most of us only use logical thinking when making a marketing decision on creativity. So this is your chance to use the whole noodle.

Take the story at the opening of this article. Let's say you listen to a creative presentation, knowing you have to pick a campaign idea. The standard way that most marketers perform this decision is to make a mental checklist and compare the ideas with their previous expectations. Then they listen just long enough to understand the ideas that are being presented.

Before the presentation is over, they have done a quick analysis against that existing checklist. Even if they react positively to an emotional idea or encounter a new direction they haven't considered, they quickly reject it. Sure, we'll laugh and make a joke about how we would never consider something that crazy.

Usually it's rejected because it doesn't match the previous expectations, or the emotion is dismissed because they start worrying how someone *else* would feel about it. They ignore their feelings and try to slow down and make a rational decision. Emotions are weak and scary, right? And a good decision maker has to quickly rank ideas and find the idea that will make the biggest impact on the numbers.

Except this process is flawed.

What's really happening is that we are forcing our executive function to overcompensate and control our subconscious. Even if we feel something, we push those feelings down and make a real decision with logic. If we only using logic to make a decision, we're not smart thinkers. We're really just shallow thinkers, using only our conscious, slow brain.

If we've learned anything from neuroscience and the brain, it's that we are making these types of decisions the wrong way. We think that we need to exercise extra effort with rational thought. But in reality, our subconscious thoughts expressed in emotion are a treasure trove of information.

After all, our prefrontal cortex can only handle a few variables, but our subconscious is much more robust.

Here's some advice from psychologist Ap Dijksterhuis on making good decisions: "Use your conscious mind to acquire all the information you need for making a decision. But don't try to analyze the information with your conscious mind. Instead, go on holiday while your unconscious mind digests it. Whatever your intuition then tells you is almost certainly going to be the best choice."[76]

That sounds a lot like the process for coming up with creative ideas. And even though many disagree with his theory of unconscious thought, there are still ways to balance both types of thinking. What if we learned from other successful agile thinkers and tried to use some of the same steps as those who discovered the big idea?

Imagine if you soaked up the presentation and data on the various campaign options. You listened with both your logical checklist and your emotions. And I mean really considered how you are feeling at every moment in the presentation. Focus on your initial reaction and your feelings after the idea has settled in. Then, instead of making a decision right there in the meeting, you gave your subconscious a chance to process it.

The decision-making process

Listen   Checklist   Incubation   Decision

You close the meeting, thanking the creative team for the ideas. And you sleep on it. Or go back to your office in a comfortable setting and focus on something else. When the time is right, you readdress the decision and see how you think and feel about it. I would imagine sometimes you may come to a different conclusion than your original expectations.

Big decisions require our emotions. Our gut. We need to access that wealth of data under the iceberg. Intuitive thinkers have mastered this process. Certainly, after training yourself to focus more on your emotions, you can make this process happen faster.

Think of famous entrepreneurs or leaders who somehow knew to zig when the world was zagging. They could recognize a big idea instantly. Probably because of the way it felt. The way they had trained their minds to process decisions in an intuitive way. They trained their dopamine sensors to react quickly when presented with good ideas. These are agile thinkers. Agile thinkers have learned to tap into their emotions and tap into that massive amount of experience and computational power.

Jonah Lehrer has a great quote on experts who have learned to use intuitive thinking.

"We tend to think of experts as being weighed down by information, their intelligence dependent on a vast amount of explicit knowledge, experts are actually profoundly intuitive. When an expert evaluates a situation, he doesn't systematically compare all the available options or consciously analyze the relevant information. He doesn't rely on elaborate spreadsheets or long lists of pros and cons. Instead, the expert naturally depends on the emotions generated by his dopamine neurons. His prediction errors have been translated into useful knowledge, which allows him to tap into a set of accurate feelings he can't begin to explain. The best experts embrace this intuitive style of thinking. They have figured out how to take advantage of their mental machinery, to steal as much wisdom as possible from their inevitable errors."[77]

In essence, if you want to get better at making marketing decisions, you need to embrace agile thinking. When we encounter complex and challenging decisions, our emotions can help us more than we think.

And just as idea generators have perfected this process, decision makers can do the same. Take in all the data. Think it through for a while. Then take a break and let your subconscious process it all. Finally, come back to the decision and pay attention to both your emotions and your logical checklist.

By training yourself to be more intuitive, you may see new connections or experience a stronger feeling on one idea over the others. You'll find that you not only feel more confident about a decision, but you also build up an expert marketing gut—a valuable asset that will help you throughout your entire career.

Strengthen our gut.

As we continue to use intuitive thinking for marketing decisions, it's only natural that we build up an intuitive mental database to match. But just as we use our executive function to guide our thoughts, we can purposefully build a database that's more robust and intuitive.

Think of the professional who has figured out her career end goal, a CEO of a midsized company. Except she takes what seems like a disconnected series of jobs. Maybe a job in sales. Then one in operations. And another in product marketing. It may seem random, but in the end, she will have built up the needed skills to perform a variety of tasks that are essential for that leadership job. Her resume will be a better match than her peers and she will be more successful at reaching the desired job. And it all starts with a thoughtful and purposeful approach.

We can also take a thoughtful approach to building up a powerful marketing intuition in our own careers. Just as we applied the creation process to creative decision making, we can connect the creative marketing pitch to building up our personal marketing gut.

Think back on the process of the basic pitch for guiding customers from first exposure to brand loyalty. The lesson is that we need both logic and emotion for a balanced approach. Why can't we use a similar process for building up our emotional database? Our lives and careers can benefit from using both, and it may help us become a more intuitive thinker.

Here's the basic pitch for a refresher:

A creative idea **stands out** with an **emotional charge** that leads to audience **participation** and greater **stickiness** that creates a **positive experience** that leads to greater **likability** that leads to repeat purchase and finally **brand loyalty**.

First, try to focus on the emotions as we encounter new experiences and ideas. Try not to shut out the possibility that an idea could work that may be different than our expectations. Think of how we can help ideas stand out in our mind. Try to create situations where we allow ideas to become an anomaly. Really, just be open minded and try to recognize the underlying emotion in experiences.

The next step is around sticky ideas and engagement. For many creative thinkers, this comes naturally as we soak in all the emotionally charged experiences around us. Many authors spend time people watching. Others keep up with pop culture. Whatever it is, notice the types of experiences that stick with us. Focus on what makes these great experiences. Why do people like a certain product? What makes a movie or book popular? Think beyond the surface to really get at the hidden truths.

Apply some the lessons from *Made to Stick* to our marketing training Look to simplify messages and marketing experiences.

Look for examples of unexpectedness in life, so we can apply similar tactics to marketing. Search for the concrete words and details in competitor messaging, so we know what nuggets will resonate with our audiences. Recognize authority in marketing tactics and apply credibility to our campaigns. Use more emotion than usual and see if we can elicit an emotional reaction from customers. And finally, become a student of storytelling. What are the elements that make stories work and how does delivery change how people engage with stories?

All of these exercises will help our ideas become stickier, and our marketing gut will build up a wealth of examples for those moments when we need to make a really important marketing decision.

The next step to become an intuitive thinker is understanding the power of likability. This can apply to our personal interactions with our team, as the more we are a likable person, the more persuasive we can be.

But we can also get a better understanding of ideas that are liked by our customers. Remember the importance of emotionally positive ideas and how that is the biggest indicator of an idea being remembered. Embrace positive experiences and look for ways that our brand can create more of them.

The more likable experiences we can create and deliver consistently, the more loyalty we can create for our personal brand. Meaning we will become more valuable to company leadership.

We should employ the same tactics we use as a marketer for our own personal work experience and our own personal brand. We want to stand out, create engaging and memorable work, and build loyalty as a business expert.

Far too often, we are like the cobbler's children. We know how to build brands for our employers, but we don't take the time to build up our personal brands. Just remember to put a little effort into building up your personal expert intuition.

Become a creative champion.

Another way to be a better marketer is to understand how to be a champion of creative ideas. After all, it takes a team to deliver big ideas to the marketplace.

There are two ways that we can become a creative champion. The first is to be able to recognize great creative ideas and help sell them up the organization and out to customers. The second is to learn how to properly give good feedback to creative teams so they can improve on their ideas.

Companies need more creative champions. Too often, we feel like we need to be the one coming up with all the big ideas. That's false. Some of the great entrepreneurs of our time didn't come up with the business idea. They just learned to recognize a good idea and then run with it.

A key ingredient of many successful design-led companies is the fact that company leadership recognizes the need for great design and ensures that it's an integral part of all business decisions. From the top down.

Whether we are the CEO of a company or the manager of a team, we can learn to be an intuitive thinker and recognize emotional ideas. Most may not change the world, but being a champion of even small creative ideas will improve our chances of business success. Look for them and do all we can to sell good ideas up our organization and out to customers.

But far too often, when faced with a choice, decision makers kill good ideas or just pick the least path of resistance. Which means we end up with bland and boring options. Instead, if we gave good feedback, the creative team would be inspired to go back and come up with better ideas.

Often, we end up giving vague feedback like, "It just doesn't feel right." Or, "Punch it up." This isn't very helpful or inspiring to a creative thinker.

We could take a lesson from the rules of engagement for feedback between authors and novelists. When they review each other's work, they never try to fix the problems, as that would limit creativity and discovery of better ideas. Instead, there are a few basic rules they use in order to give the author the maximum chance of improving the work.

They simply describe how they felt as they were reading a certain section. They give specific information about their *feelings*. Like, "I was confused in this paragraph and didn't understand the connection." Or perhaps, "During this part I was bored and lost interest."

Feedback like this to a creative person helps them understand what is going wrong in an experience, so they can go back and find ways to improve it. Maybe they need a new photo that's more engaging. Or a better transition between paragraphs of a story.

When giving feedback about creative ideas, don't limit the options by being too prescriptive. Express how you *felt*, which is a good indication of whether the idea is lighting up your brain or not. Then the creative can go back and discover a new way to express the idea, so that it will resonate.

Keep in mind that there are many ways to express an idea. Trust the team. And don't forget to provide positive feedback of the things you do like. This helps them know what is working so they can create more moments like that one.

Of course, I'm not trying to paint a utopian picture of feedback. If the idea is boring or unemotional and you feel nothing, express that as well. The more we think about the emotional impact of marketing ideas, the better we can work together to create better ideas. Help others become a creative champion as well.

Good decisions require good emotions.

In today's marketing world, where budgets are constantly shrinking, we have to do more with less. Why wouldn't you use the best options to create a customer experience that positively impacts the bottom line? It's the logical option.

When you're sitting at that conference-room table and you're listening to someone present a new idea, make sure to listen with your emotions as much as you do with your checklist. Give your subconscious time to process, so you can make more intuitive decisions.

Don't be ruled by emotion. But don't be ruled by a lack of emotion. It's a tough balance to learn how to embrace and control your emotions. Become an intuitive thinker.

The more you practice becoming an intuitive thinker, the better you will become as a marketing decision maker. Become a student of experiences and look for ways to incorporate those learnings into your strategies. Really, this is how creative people become good at coming up with big ideas. You train your brain to notice anomalies and you get faster at making new emotional connections. If you're a logical thinker, you can be methodical about these choices, or make it an organic experience like most creative types.

Regardless, the outcome will be the same. You'll be better at recognizing and championing good ideas. And you'll build up a big database of subconscious ideas that you can use to become a marketing superstar. It's a logical strategy about becoming more in tune with your emotions.

Because deep down, emotion is really what makes us logical.

Chapter 14

HOW TO MEASURE CREATIVE IDEAS

Tyler England has been measuring marketing ideas for more than fifteen years. As the vice president of customer and marketing insights and strategy at HP, he was charged with understanding every detail concerning HP's customers and finding the insights that turn customer loyalty into sales.

When I spoke with him about how he approaches this process, he understood a balanced approach. "When measuring creative ideas, the debate is often around which system should weigh heavier—the more automatic and emotional system or the more rational and deliberate system."[78]

Over the years that England has spent studying the topic of creative measurement, he's learned that judging the success of creative ideas isn't always black and white. Even with a tremendous amount of data and modern techniques, the data can quickly get muddy. It turns out, measurement requires as much intuitive thinking as coming up with the original ideas.

Here's how England explains it: "Stakeholders often want a definitive answer on a certain piece of creative. They assume that because we conduct a research project, we should have all the answers. But the true answer is that it depends. There are so many factors to weigh, and people don't always respond to research in a rational manner. They hide their emotions. In order to get more clear answers, we have to nail both the System 1 and System 2 thinking of our customers. System 1 helps with engagement and memory, while System 2 helps translate it all into action and purchase. And arguably, System 1, or the emotional system, is increasingly the gatekeeper to System 2."[79]

England understands that measurement isn't limited to logic and rational thought. You don't just ask a question and record the answer. It's extremely emotional as well. And we have to use other techniques to understand people's emotional responses. Techniques based on behavioral economics and human psychology.

He's used every method available over the years, but lately he finds that the best research companies use multiple measurement methods to understand both systems.

Companies like Millward Brown and BrainJuicer are two examples of research testing firms that have partnered with HP because they have proprietary methods to measure both emotive and rational systems. They did base testing on many of the same insights shared by behavioral economists such as Kahneman, Thaler, and Ariely.

"Their tests are designed to isolate the creative, rather than throw it directly into an in-market A/B test, which can muddy the results with other executional and targeting factors. For instance, I like BrainJuicer's use of an emotive scale based on facial expressions to capture a System 1 response. It may not be perfect, but it forces a response a bit more toward an emotional reaction. Then they follow it up with a logical survey with questions to capture more of a rational response."[80]

In the past, much of research ignored the emotional half of our responses. It tried to stay as rational as possible with very direct and precise questions. The problem, similar to focus groups, is that respondents put on a different face when asked to answer. They slowed down and only used their logical brains to solve the research questions. But today, now that we better understand how we think, we work toward getting results that question both systems.

We need more measurement and research that understands and follows this balanced approach. Unfortunately, because of cost, this type of research is typically reserved for the high-cost, higher-risk, anchor creative of a campaign.

But that doesn't mean we can't apply the learnings from the big research projects on a balanced approach with everyday testing. Overall, England feels that research testing should focus on metrics around four universal truths in order to figure out the right balance for each brand.

"Working with some of the lead thinkers and agencies on this subject, combined with observing this stuff for years, there are several universal truths that need to be followed. These four are: emotive, convincingness, connection to the product, and branding."[81]

Emotive helps with breakthrough and is key to retaining a memory about the experience. *Convincingness* is the rational side of things and helps with differentiation and understanding the benefits. A strong *connection to the product* is needed by making sure the product or service is baked into the message, as this helps drive purchase interest and connects the emotion and logic to the brand memory. And finally, *branding* is always important so that you have a strong anchor or location to file the memory, otherwise the brand doesn't benefit from both short-term and long-term memory credit—that ultimately translates into loyalty.

It's exciting to see companies put an equal amount of emphasis on both sides of the equation in order to get more human results. And when we tie these universal truths back to neuroscience and how we consume content, create memories, store memories, and recall those impressions, it gives us a more balanced approach to really understanding how effective creative ideas can be.

Agile versus waterfall.

Some may question why we spend any resources on creative measurement. Because at the end of the day, isn't sales or the bottom line the ultimate judge of the success of an idea?

And with the advances in data-driven marketing, do all these other methods still have a purpose? Can't we just measure our ideas through the many types of digital and customer analytics and get a real answer on what is effective or not?

The answer is, it depends. Certainly, there is no debate that sales are the final word for a company's success. At least for those businesses who are looking for a profit. But when it comes to measurement, there are many factors to consider, and having an understanding of all methods is important. Otherwise, you are simply focused on one strategy and one point of view on effectiveness.

For example, there are many companies that want insight on an idea long before it become a sales statistic. They may have long sales cycles, and by the time a sale happens, they've already made the gamble. So they are looking for insight early in the process. They want quick insights so they can adjust the plan.

If we've learned from recent lessons of web production, taking a more agile approach, rather than a waterfall approach, is the best way to succeed.

With an agile approach, you try something, test it, analyze the results, discover the insights, then go back and try some more. You're constantly iterating, tweaking, prototyping, and learning as you go.

If you use a waterfall approach, you build the whole thing and then see how it turns out. You may find that you've spent a ton of time and money working on the wrong features. Just looking at sales results can be a waterfall approach. Often, it's too late to do anything about it and you haven't learned much about what isn't working.

There are also other companies that use more organic and non-digital communication methods. Maybe the best advertising for that company is a billboard, but they don't have instant metrics to measure how effective the billboard is for their sales. And even though many of us claim to have analytics on non-digital media, there are still limitations. We can certainly measure sales spikes and attribute them to offline media, but when calculating lift in a campaign, it can quickly get fuzzy.

Finally, as England mentioned previously, there are so many things to measure, we often muddy the water in terms of really knowing the result of research and testing. For a day-to-day insight, an A/B test may be ideal. But it needs to be very specific, or it may confuse more than guide. When approaching a test, we need to be very careful of the scope and variables in the test.

Over the years, I've worked with teams and vendors on a variety of testing methods. Some of these projects include everything from user testing, in-market A/B tests, multi-variate tests, heat mapping, message testing, individual interviews, and even eye tracking systems that date back to the mid 1990s when digital was emerging.

Many of these methods offer very specific benefits. For example, user testing for a website helps us know if customers can figure out the UX and if they are clicking the things we want them to click. It's not testing their opinions or feelings. It's simply discovering details about the user experience. Many users may express their feelings on design, but that emotional response is usually just a sign of their confusion or frustrations on certain design elements or flow.

And even with very linear testing like this, you can easily lead the witness to get them to talk or respond to things that they wouldn't have explored on their own. Or you can get a false positive result. The environment you choose, the questions you ask, the guidance you give can all affect the outcome of the data. Many of these methods are observational science. And that doesn't always give us insight into how a person is really thinking.

In essence, data on its own isn't everything. It isn't the final word. And you shouldn't put all your faith on one type of testing. Use all methods at your disposal, including your gut, to get an idea of how effective your ideas really are. And remember that testing requires systematic results from multiple experiments. The beauty of getting answers to our hypothesis is testing, but it takes work.

Data isn't all powerful. It needs help. The software you use, the analysts, the people who take action—all these variables can change the outcome. It's still a very human endeavor. The data-driven robots haven't taken over the world, even though many people act like robots are firmly in charge and that this process has been perfected.

Data and creative ideas must work together. Data inspires ideas and ideas are proven out with data. As Ryan Pizzuto put it, "All testing starts with a bright idea, but you need to validate those ideas with data."[82]

I've had many conversations with fellow marketers who say something like, "We tested creative ideas with our operational emails and we got a better result with straightforward facts. So emotional ideas don't work."

Again, keep in mind that this is a very limited test and point of view. One or even several A/B tests aren't the ultimate truth. Especially when testing highly emotional things such as a subject line or headline.

Your results may show that a direct headline worked best. But consider this—was the fact or stat you used emotionally charged? Or perhaps the audience had already built up enough loyalty through previous creative experiences with the brand. They were willing to give up a little emotional capital to get a specific job done quickly.

There are so many factors in every subjective piece of communication that a single or a few A/B tests aren't able to give you holistic answers on something as massive as the effectiveness of creative ideas.

Or perhaps that specific test is correct, and in an operational email deep in the funnel, customers aren't interested in emotional ideas. But a boring and direct message may be totally off brand. And that email could benefit from a bit of brand personality to keep the loyalty strong.

There are many tactics that aren't emotional or creative but still work effectively. Bad ideas still work. Couponing works, but that doesn't mean certain brands should use it. Couponing could ultimately destroy a brand and make it a commodity product based on cost rather than a premium brand based on an emotional appeal. So even if you test something and get a certain result, that doesn't mean it's the right thing to do.

Don't take all data as ultimate truth. We learn a little with each test. Even if we connect all our customers up to an fMRI machine, we would learn some insights. But because of the environment, we may lose some truth as well. Advocate a more holistic and balanced approach to learn as much as we can about subjective ideas in order to know what will work better.

Just because a measurement tactic sounds scientific and digital, that doesn't mean it's all-encompassing (and our cultures place a premium on anything that seems super rational). Remember, it's a tool. There are many tools we can and should use. But keep a balanced approach when measuring creative ideas.

For far too long, we have based measurement of creative ideas with only a rational approach. But humans react in both rational and emotional ways. Let's take advantage of what neuroscience has taught us recently and find ways to incorporate emotional testing as well.

Data-driven measurement.

Even though I just blasted some testing methods, data really is critical. And anyone who doesn't see the value in data-driven marketing is certain to fail. But data, just like everything in life, has a place and a specific benefit.

Data drives marketing. It offers insight we haven't had in past decades. It lets us know what efforts are working. It gives us knowledge about our customers unlike ever before. It empowers our ideas. And it's a catalyst to great marketing.

But it isn't the end-all. It's part of the experience. And in today's economy where the whole experience is what will differentiate companies, the data is just the beginning.

Data is the driving force, but experiences still need to be crafted by great ideas. Data on its own is just ones and zeros. It takes sophisticated software and human intuition to turn that data into deep insight.

At a recent Adobe Summit, Robert Rose spoke with Zann Aeck, the director of digital marketing at NetApp. She offered a realistic perspective on the role of data in marketing.

"Eons ago, marketing was really about a lot of assumptions and trying to create an experience that people wanted to be part of. When you get into data-driven marketing, you know whether or not people are actually responding."[83]

Marketing funnels are typically full of assumptions based on past metrics. So really, one role of data driven marketing is to eliminate those guesses. When you make marketing decisions, you are basing them on real responses. Which means we can eliminate the guesswork and create better experiences.

"Data-driven marketing for NetApp is really about providing context to all the data, learning from the data, and making better, less risky decisions. There's no more assumptions that you need to bring into it from a marketing perspective. It's not about what your boss likes, what your CMO likes, or what your CEO likes. These days it's about the data. The data will prove exactly what's going to happen."[84]

Aeck knows that data is critical. Marketing is subjective, and we need to know what our customers think. But it's also not the magic bullet. We just need to understand the role it plays and not overlook the need for creative ideas, too. It's all about context.

"Data is meaningless until you have context around it. And even with website traffic, email downloads, opens, click-throughs, all that stuff . . . when you take a look at that data, and all this anonymous data at that, trying to understand the context and what's working and what's not is a hard nut to crack. And so, I think that's part of the big challenge of understanding the experience that you're creating. And then, of course, how do you measure that? How do you really understand that there's something engaging about that experience that people are doing from that digital perspective?

"No one wants to read a white paper, you know, so you do need to take a look at how are you making it interesting, the experience and the connection with the, dare I say it, brand is still really critical even though when they shut down after work and they're heading home, the last thing that they want to do is read about data storage."[85]

For NetApp, Acek understands the need for balance. We need to think about the customer experience and give them engaging moments, based on data and measurement. We can't just dump data on our customers or they will leave. When it comes to measuring our marketing today, with data we have many more definitive answers. But again, we need to balance both types of thinking.

A simple solution to measure emotion.

One of the first questions that I get after presenting on this topic is, "How do I know if my ideas have the right emotion?"

We have data and analytics. But this won't tell us if the idea has enough emotion or the right emotion. We discussed how some companies like Millward Brown and BrainJuicer are creating systems to test both logic and emotion. But how do you know in the moment if an idea has enough emotion?

Fortunately, we are at an interesting time where many companies are just figuring out better ways to do this. There are new startups experimenting on interesting ways to quickly measure our emotional responses. One example is Lightwave.

Rana June, the CEO of Lightwave, describes their company as a pioneer in emotion technology, where emotion tech is the collection of bio feedback and analysis of that data in support of a marketing metric. In other words, they use a variety of smart tech to measure our feelings.

"If emotion is the currency of experience," Rana explains, "then there needs to be a way to describe that and validate that we are effective at creating it. Emotion tech could be anything from facial recognition, to bio feedback from things like heart rate, or any other emotion metric like ambient measurement such as thermal imaging or audio detection. There are a lot of ways that you can start to derive signals from the body that can help to tell that story."[86]

Lightwave's measurement experience is impressive. In real time, they can chart your emotions as you watch a video in a dark room. Your emotional spikes and valleys are recorded on a large screen, painted in a colorful wave that represents the type and power of the emotions you feel at specific moments while watching the video. Through data visualization, clients can instantly see when people are reacting emotionally, and how strong the emotion is at any moment.

Unfortunately, these amazing research tools aren't cheap. Most companies don't have unlimited budgets to test every little ad or billboard with emotion technology.

If money were no object, we would all connect our customers to an fMRI machine and watch for brainwave patterns. But it's not economically feasible.

When others ask me how to measure emotions, they're typically asking for a quick solution that they can use every day. Something they can do with limited budget.

So, here's a simple solution based on a study by Paul J Zak, the founding director of the Center for Neuroeconomic Studies at Claremont Graduate University.

Zak is known as the father of neuroeconomics. He's made a career out of connecting neuroscience to finance, or more particularly, the science behind what makes people spend money.

In his article titled, "Why inspiring stories make us react: the neuroscience of narrative," he explains an experiment where he discovered a simple formula for predicting spending behavior based on an emotional connection.

"Narratives that cause us to pay attention and also involve us emotionally are the stories that move us to action."[87]

Here's that statement represented as a simple formula:

Why stories make us react

Attention ➕ *Emotion* ═ *Action*

Zak was able to isolate these two key ingredients in creative stories that drive us to action. And by action, he measured if people were willing to pay money after each experiment, so we could see the correlation between the formula and motivating people to spend money.

The first ingredient is attention. In the lab, he tested attention by measuring a quickened heartbeat and sweat from the eccrine glands in the skin. Attention is critical because our brains treat it as a scarce resource that needs to be conserved, as it is metabolically expensive.

The second ingredient is emotion. This proved more challenging to measure in real time. He knew that the neurochemical in question was oxytocin. In a previous study, his lab showed that oxytocin is the regulator of prosocial behavior. Like having pride in others or being more emotionally engaged with the characters in a story. They found that the more oxytocin that is present in a person, the more willing they are to feel connected and act on that connection.

Zak found his eureka moment with the vagus nerve. Rather than measuring levels of oxytocin in the blood after the experience, he could measure the flow of oxytocin in real-time from the vagus nerve.

By measuring these two ingredients, attention and emotion, Zak was able to track millisecond by millisecond as a person watched a video. In the end, they could predict if a person would give money with an 82 percent accuracy, based on how much attention and emotion were present.

We may not have the time or money to test our marketing in an electrocardiogram (ECG) lab like Paul Zak. But we can learn a lot from his experiments.

Here's a simple way to use Zak's insight without going to the lab.

A simple way to measure

    A. Insights   *(Use data to establish triggers.)*

    B. Create experience   *(Anomaly + Empathy.)*

    C. Measure   *(Does experience hit triggers?)*

First, discover an insight about your audience. Use your analytics, focus groups, research, surveys, all the logical measurement tactics to discover data about your customer. (This is the appropriate way to use these logical tools, not with testing creative ideas.) Find out the emotional triggers that matter to them. What are the hot topics? What do they like? What do they want or care about? This is the time to put on your logical hat. You want to use these traditional tools to *discover* the emotion, not *measure* it.

Once you have the insights into what emotional triggers will connect with your audience, the next step is to create the experience. This is the creative process where you use those insights and wrap them in a story or art or a video. But as you create the experience, make sure you are using that insight, or anomaly, as the focal point. Then give that anomaly as much emotional juice as possible.

Finally, and here's where the actual measurement comes in, you simple compare your creative idea back to the data insight.

Does the idea hit the emotional trigger?

Does the idea pull on our emotions?

Does A = B?

If the answer is yes to both of these questions, then you can be confident that the creative idea will resonate with your audience.

It may not be accurate to 85 percent, but the same principles apply. You don't need to hook your customer up to an electrocardiogram. You just need to make sure it's something they will pay attention to (anomaly) and have an emotional connection with (empathy). It can be that simple.

Hard numbers for a soft experience.

A reason that many marketers feel that creativity is more of a softer priority is because often, the measurements and data that we use in our industry to express results and success are hard numbers.

Marketers and sales express success in terms of metrics—ROI, clicks, engagement numbers, lifetime value, and other KPIs. Most marketing funnels are based on numbers, with formulas connected to every step of journey. We turn leads into MQLs and SALs.

The numbers often lead us toward a more logical approach to marketing. We think that the only way to prove our success is through hard facts. Naturally, this makes us think that everything in the process should be tied to numbers.

But as we move toward an experience economy, where companies want to know the ROI of emotional experiences, more marketers are asking how we measure creative experiences. In an interview with Robert Rose, thought leader Paul Greenberg, of the 57 Group, said that this is a real challenge, but it is possible.

"Most marketing departments aren't setup for right brain thinking. They are more focused on transactions, pushing product out to customers. They need to focus on how customers behave and feel. Only then will they create experiences that really push ROI.

Today marketing is being held accountable more and more for revenue goals. This makes them panic and want to go back to science and transactions. Hard numbers. But the way to succeed is to go for the higher goal of experience marketing, which is softer."[88]

Admittedly, this is a real challenge. It's hard to ignore the numbers and base your success on intangible ideas. But Greenberg also gives us hope that we can tie these softer benefits to the bottom line.

"You have to show ROI. But it exists. You have to tie a whole journey to the purchase, not just the last step. Start with data driven, learn insights, find stickiness within experiences, and tie the whole story together. It's not just a business case to say we can get more revenue, but an efficiency argument and a value add. We can do more for less.

"To retain customers, you need to create experiences where they feel it. That's what marketers need to create at every moment along the journey."[89]

There is value in connecting creativity to profits. But with marketing departments so entrenched in hard numbers, we need to somehow make a change. I'm not suggesting we swing the pendulum all the way in the opposite direction. The message of this book is to find balance.

What if marketing plans included an objective to create an impactful idea, a campaign, or find an insight? And then we tie that insight to the overall success of the journey. Because at the end of the day, we are just measuring ourselves against a success metric. But this metric could be a simple goal. Something like finding a great emotional trigger for a certain audience. Or figuring out what type of experience will resonate with our customers. Then add a number to a response mechanism through analytics, surveys, or measurable goals. We can still have other strategies and tactics that focus on concrete metrics, but to ensure we prioritize creativity, we can keep it on the master plan.

Marketing shouldn't just be about the analytics. It's also the human insights we get from the numbers. As we build marketing plans, we should include a lift factor based on creative insight. Creative ideas that include world-class design and emotional copy create a likable lift factor. As described by Du Plessis, this creative lift factor becomes a multiplier for your metrics.

The way to champion ideas is to make them part of our process and measurement. If not, they're more easily forgotten, and we fall back into the habit of number crunching and logic. This is not only important for marketing plans, but as we watch how design-led companies are thriving, this becomes equally important for business plans and company culture.

As more companies understand the value of experiences—emotional moments created for customers—we'll find more ways to create the right balance of KPIs that include creative ideas. This is new territory. But taking some time during annual planning to recognize measurable creative goals for your company will go a long way. The only way to make change is to start somewhere.

Creative goals may require the creative team.

Here's a great starting point—make the creative team care equally about marketing metrics. In a world where data and art have equal seats at the business decision table, creative departments should understand essential KPIs and should work to lift those numbers.

Steve Gustavson, an executive creative director at Adobe, feels passionate about this fact. "Far too often, only the marketing team feels the responsibility of hitting a number every quarter. But honestly, everyone in the company should feel the accountability—including the creative team. When crafting art or copy, they should understand the need to balance creativity and results in order to do their part to build the company. It takes both sides working toward a common goal."[90]

If we could get creative directors to care about the metrics and marketers to care about emotional ideas, we improve our chances for business success. Don't get so hung up in the math that we forget the art.

And because creative directors understand the creative process and the value of emotional experiences, it only makes sense that they will have a good idea of how to measure the right emotions for their company. So put the creative department to work in figuring out what measurable goals to add to the annual marketing plan.

The challenge we should embrace is discovering what emotion is right for each audience and how we can use that to better connect with each individual. This is something that the numbers typically don't tell us. Certainly, with advanced analytics solutions we can better predict what this may be. But often it comes down to human insight.

No wonder companies who find a person with an exceptional talent at discovering insights and who can easily make these emotional connections are retained and well compensated.

Organizations that rely only on numbers and metrics for marketing strategies are just as limited as companies that don't embrace design-led principles. And with the new perspective on companies embracing experience-led strategies, the art side of the equation is even more important.

The need for balance of both art and science in all aspects of business and marketing is essential. In the digital era, we are consuming more and more data about our customers. But data alone won't improve sales. It's the addition of emotional insight that will affect our actions.

Balanced metrics.

When we measure our emotional ideas, we won't find the right answers if we only take a rational approach. The takeaway here is to use a variety of methods that appeal to both logical and emotional systems. Use a balanced approach to measurement.

You can use both data and experience to make an informed decision. If the data doesn't feel right, there's a reason. Chances are, you're getting a data-filled emotional response from your subconscious. Look for other ways to test and find a unique perspective or insight.

In the end, we have many more ways to measure ideas with digital. But a balanced approach for testing creative ideas allows us to trust our guts and learn from our peers, while still measuring actual results with customer analytics.

Every great customer experience should appeal to both rational and emotional systems. So it makes sense that we should test and measure our ideas with techniques that understand both systems as well.

Chapter 15

A BALANCED APPROACH TO AWARD SHOWS AND FOCUS GROUPS

It was supposed to be a special award for professionals. Each year at the award show for best advertising in Utah, known as the Addys, one piece of marketing is singled out as the people's choice award.

The top talent from advertising agencies, production firms, film houses, and company marketing departments come for an evening of networking and celebrating the best creative ideas for the past year.

As part of the event, all the professionals who are present at the show vote on the single best piece of work to win the people's choice award. The traveling trophy is an oversized golden wrestling belt that is put on display at the winning company for a year, and then is awarded to a new company at the next award gala.

A few years ago, I was the president of the American Advertising Federation of Utah, the trade organization that sponsors the Addy Awards. In the past, we'd hand around ballots to the audience and then tally up the votes during the presentation.

But that year, we thought we would try a new form of voting. Rather than hand out old-school paper ballots, we used a texting system where the audience could text in their vote for the best idea. We had a live dashboard projected on a big screen for everyone to watch.

As the voting began, there were a few TV spots and several pieces of marketing collateral jockeying for first place. We gave the audience ten minutes to cast their vote, assuming some of those who had never texted in a vote like this may need some time to figure it out.

Suddenly in the last two minutes, a flood of votes poured in for a student entry. A student entry. We didn't even think it qualified, as this was an award for professionals. But the votes for the student work overwhelmed everything else and left the professionals in the dust.

When we closed the voting, we were unsure how this had happened. There were only a handful of students in the audience. Did the professionals really like the student idea better?

As the award show continued, those of us behind the scenes who ran the award show gathered to discuss what had happened. Some complained that it wasn't fair for a student to win, as their work didn't have to live up to the rigor of clients and stakeholders. They just produced spec work about whatever they wanted.

In the end, we decided to uphold the vote and allowed the student to accept the people's choice award on behalf of his university. With everyone having watched the results on the big screen, we felt it would cause more of a problem by disqualifying the student entry.

Later, after the show ended, we looked at the data in the texting software. We noticed that most of the votes came from a different area code. It was the city for the winning student entry where the university was located.

We asked one of the students who was still mingling at the after-party. She told us that the students had found out about the texting vote for the people's choice and had setup a texting tree with a huge group of students back at the university. Once they knew what number to use for the vote, they spread the word and had students back home join in.

We were shocked. The students had gamed the system. They found a loophole and had exploited it to their advantage. Our plan for accurate crowdsourcing had backfired.

All that glitters is good?

This experience highlights an important question. How do you know if a creative idea is really a good idea?

And I'm not talking about how to measure creative work against marketing KPIs. That's a discussion of effectiveness. We discussed measurement in the last chapter. I'm talking about how to know for yourself if a message or idea is emotional enough or hitting the right emotional triggers to matter. How do we know a good idea when we see it?

For the first decade of my career in advertising, the easy answer was it's good if it wins an award. In the '90s, creative careers were made and lost based on the big advertising award shows.

Communication Arts. The One Show. The Radio Mercury Awards. The Obbies. The Addys. The Athenas. The Clios. The Cannes Lions. The D&AD. The Effies. The AIGA 100. The Webbys. And the list goes on and on.

Advertising agencies were the most aggressive for these awards, as the recognition would prove that you were legitimate and creative. Which in theory would attract more clients and more profits. And for years, this was true.

But as recessions hit and budgets shrank, fewer could afford to enter work into all the award shows. In addition, around 2001 before the dot-com bubble burst, there was a slew of creative campaigns that flooded the market. These campaigns were creative but had little connection to the products they advertised. Many complained that agencies were just creating work for the award shows, not to sell products for their clients.

This caused a big backlash, and some advertisers debated the value of award shows. It reverted back to the classic debate—is it about creativity or results? In response, a few award shows changed tactics and focused on awarding creative ideas that proved sales results of some sort. And some ad agencies used anti-award show tactics as a new business model to attract clients who wanted real work, not the shallow stuff that award-winning agencies would display on their lobby shelves.

Typically, award shows recruit several talented judges who have proved that they know good creative work. They have a strong creative advertising gut as they have been exposed to years of good and bad creative ideas. These judges spend a few days looking at thousands and thousands of pieces of advertising and marketing and select the best of the best, according to a range of criteria.

It's been a solid way of judging creative ideas for decades. But is it still the best way to judge creative ideas?

Behind the scenes, I saw a different perspective on the process of judging. For ten years, I helped manage award shows for the AAF in Utah and the western district.

When the judges are overloaded with thousands of ideas and several days of judging, far too often I saw that they ended up choosing ideas from categories that were easier to judge. After all, they are human and their brains were overloaded. After so many hours of judging, they often leaned toward more immersive mediums and ideas that indexed more on entertainment than intellect.

For example, TV spots and video were often at the top of the list, where a smart brochure or B2B offering received less love. And don't put your hopes on radio or web banner ads as they barely got a few milliseconds of attention.

One year, I tried to keep the judges focused on radio. Rather than have them sit in a conference room and try to focus on the radio spots, we went for a drive. I put them all in a large SUV and drove around town while they listened to the radio finalists. The good news is that they had a change in scenery and were alert. The bad news is they still gave each radio spot about two seconds before asking me to skip to the next one.

My point is that certain mediums were over-indexed, and many ideas were given less time than what a typical consumer would offer your messages. Every judge has certain biases, and we noticed how different the best work would be year in and year out based on the personal style and background skills of the judge. If they were a designer, the more pure designs won. If they were a writer, more headline-driven ads won.

Also, some of the personalities of judges were so overbearing that they influenced the other judges' decisions (just like a focus group) or their individual scores changed the whole outcome of the award show. (Like one judge who gave almost everything less than five out of one hundred except a few pieces.) Add to that the fact that some judges are caught up in all the PR and social awareness of certain campaigns, making them rise to the top because they are already top of mind.

My takeaway is that there are some positives and negatives of the current process. Hands down, I feel that the best judges of creative ideas are those who have fought in the arena to create big ideas themselves.

If you've ever heard this famous Teddy Roosevelt quote, it summarizes my thoughts perfectly. "It is not the critic who counts; not the man who points out how the strong man stumbles, or where the doer of deeds could have done them better. The credit belongs to the man who is actually in the arena, whose face is marred by dust and sweat and blood; who strives valiantly; who errs, who comes up short again and again, because there is no effort without error and shortcoming; but who does actually strive to do the deeds; who knows great enthusiasms, the great devotions; who spends himself in a worthy cause; who at the best knows in the end the triumph of high achievement, and who at the worst, if he fails, at least fails while daring greatly, so that his place shall never be with those cold and timid souls who neither know victory nor defeat."[91]

In short, the best judge is a peer. Not someone from the cheap seats. And this idea of peers being the best judges has also been the conclusion of a more recent scientific study.

Justin M Berg, of the Stanford Graduate School of Business, conducted research to learn the best way to forecast the success of novel ideas. He worked with both professionals and consumers in a study involving more than thirteen thousand people.

According to Berg, "Results suggest that creators were more accurate than managers when forecasting about others' novel ideas (but not their own ideas).

"In essence, this research suggests that the best judges of others' ideas in organizations may be those who are busy generating their own ideas."[92]

This follows the pattern in previous chapters about training our brains to be more sensitive to emotions and accustomed to intuitive thinking.

Certainly, for award shows, the peer expert review is an important element. But if we are only judging marketing based on creativity, what about the logical side? Most award shows only take into consideration the emotions, how do we also judge the logical aspects of a campaign? After all, strategy and creativity are both important.

A focus group of one.

For decades, the answer to judging ideas from the logical side of the house has been focus groups. It feels so logical and scientific. I mean, you're sitting behind a one-way mirror looking at real people. That has to be clinical.

Unfortunately, there have been many blog articles and books that suggest that focus groups are the worst when it comes to understanding the emotional needs of customers. Focus groups only focus on logic.

Psychologist Mark Ingwer, in his book *Empathetic Marketing*, talks about how customers have deep emotional needs and that companies must satisfy these emotional needs in order to build relationships and brand loyalty. He talks about how we measure customer satisfaction and how logical methods such as focus groups or customer surveys don't get at the heart of emotional responses.

"This is a problem for businesses using a logical, traditional process to study an emotional issue of satisfaction—an approach that cannot readily deliver the accurate emotional insights required. It's a problem of perspective. If a business is going to learn about an emotional issue, it needs to study the issue with a method that is sensitive to emotion. At the end of the day, businesses must see their customers as individuals always striving for a healthy sense of self-identity.

"When people find a product or service that transcends the generic 'satisfaction' benchmark, it's gratifying for the consumer, and in turn, a positive for the company that provided it. Yet when a company fails to respond to the needs buried in the consumer psyche—or worse yet, decides for the consumer what he or she needs—the product, service, or brand can be a disappointment instead of a delight, frustrating the consumer and impeding his or her achievement of the ideal sense of self."[93]

Using research to find out if customers are satisfied or if the product tests well is only scratching the surface. Ingwer notes that customer satisfaction is used by 90 percent of companies as a success benchmark. But these surveys use a logical response, asking the customer to analyze or rate their satisfaction score. To do this, they focus on their slow system and come up with a logical answer.

When we look at the model of focus groups from a brain perspective, we can see plenty of weakness. People are trying to solve your problems, so they may ignore their emotional system and focus really hard on giving a logical answer. They ignore their intuition. They try to think about how others are thinking. Or they may ignore logic and only use emotion. They are easily influenced by loud people in the group. In short, they aren't in their right minds. They are in a completely different mindset of a normal consumer situation.

To overcome many of the issues of focus groups, researchers try instead to have campfire chats with just a few people. They try to make it comfortable for subjects to really express how they feel. But it's just not as accurate as we would like.

Or we test creative concepts rather than real work, to get an idea of which messaging direction is better to follow. But again, people in these groups aren't reacting naturally to the ideas. They're trying to solve your problems because you're giving them cash or a gift card. They are thinking about the process and outcome, rather than their emotional reaction to the message.

There are many who feel that focus groups make sense for certain types of research goals. And I can concede that every research method may have unique advantages. You may find broad guidance. But not definitive answers. We need to be careful of hard facts based on this approach.

Focus groups should not be used to draw conclusions. Or to prove that a product or campaign will succeed. If you are hoping that a focus group will help you judge whether an idea is good or not, you will be disappointed. If you have other research goals, then I will step down from the soapbox. My intent is simply to know the best way to judge creative ideas.

Boaty McBoatface.

For many, the holy grail answer to this problem was the introduction of crowdsourcing. Let the people decide. Give consumers the chance to judge what is creative and worth saying.

With the rise of the web and the introduction of social platforms, marketers had a new way to drastically increase the reach and speed of research. They could use crowdsourcing to get instant feedback from their audiences.

The allure of crowdsourcing is getting an answer directly from your audience. Companies send out a brief survey to people who fit their target. Or they get on social media and ask a question with a simple survey. The data they get back should be a clear indication of the market's desires, right? Why guess at what they want when you can just ask them and get a direct answer?

Crowdsourcing has been so hot in the past few years, we saw brand new agencies be established on this principle. One of the more famous is Victors and Spoils.[94] Their story focuses on the fact that they don't know everything. But they're smart enough to know when to tap into the rest of the planet. Sure, creative teams can be smart and try to put themselves in the shoes of others. But why not just go directly to the source. Then they combine all the good from the crowd with their expertise. Which turns good advertising into great advertising.

Victors and Spoils uses a hybrid approach, which helps them retain some control of the outcome. For many other companies who have embraced the pure form of crowdsourcing, where they give the ownership to the people, it doesn't always work out the way they want.

For example, as we learned in the opening story of this chapter, you can often get results that are adversely influenced by a few rather than an accurate result from the many. A few students altered the true winner in the people's choice award. In addition, you may get results that are completely opposite of what your brand is all about.

One example of this is the naming of a new UK polar research vessel.[95] In the spirit of good PR, the British public were allowed to vote on the new name for the £200 million ship. The winning name, by a landslide, was Boaty McBoatface. However, the government didn't feel like that was a name becoming of a serious research vessel. So instead, they chose the fourth-place name, the RSS Sir David Attenborough.

The Internet and social platforms were outraged over the decision. After all, the government had given them the control and had asked the public to do the naming job. When the control was taken back, Twitter and Facebook were on fire with angry comments. The crowd turned on their master. They considered it a democratic breach. Other companies jumped on board to show how they support the public. Like Bjorn Baker's team at Sydney's Warwick Farm racecourse that named a racehorse "Horsey McHorseface" in homage to the scandal.

As other groups have turned to crowdsourcing, they try to qualify their ask, so that their good faith doesn't turn into another Boaty McBoatface fiasco.

This issue isn't singular to naming competitions. Online contests, polls, or any experience where people have an opportunity to gain something are open to disaster. When you give up control, you can't take it back.

Another problem with just letting the crowd go wild is that it can be influenced easily by anyone who has an agenda. Like the people's choice Addy event with the student takeover, you also have to be aware that people are gaming the system. If the whole purpose of crowdsourcing is to get an accurate measure of public opinion, you need to be careful that you're getting accurate results. Or that a few loud voices aren't spoiling all the data. Very similar to the problems we face as marketers with focus groups.

Is crowdsourcing the answer to our creative judging problems? Maybe. Sure, there are some inherent dangers to consider, but if you can keep them in control, you're still getting a powerful instant gut check from your audience.

A balanced approach.

Before working for Adobe, I attended the Adobe MAX creativity conference in Los Angeles. In one of the keynote presentations, Scott Belsky, one of the founders of Behance, made an interesting announcement that made me sit up straight in my seat.[96]

Behance is a creative community website where creative professionals around the globe can create online portfolios and share their best work. More than that, it creates a creative marketplace where clients and creatives can connect.

Businesses can browse all the portfolios to find the ideal talent for their job. Behance removes all the layers and bureaucracy between the two groups and offers equal access to every creative person to make a name for themselves.

Up to this point, the way that designers and artists gained popularity was through a form of crowdsourcing. Anyone in the community could up vote a talented artist so that they rose higher in the searches and rankings. It was a pure crowd play, where the control was in the hands of the people.

And then Belsky announced that this system would be changing. Rather than just rely on the crowd to dictate whose work was good, Behance would add in a layer of peer review. Experts in the various fields would also vote on which portfolios and projects were considered great. But the vote of these judges would count more than an individual member of the creative community.

Back then, as I was contemplating the best way to judge creative work, I found this change fascinating. To me, Behance was admitting that giving complete control to the crowd wasn't the best answer. I don't know the reason for the change. I can only speculate that some were gaming the system to get more visibility.

By including a peer judge layer, Behance was taking the good of crowdsourcing and the benefits of award show judges and creating a mix of both concepts. This allowed the audience to have a vote, but peer judges who are experts in the field could course correct and help guide the community to a better conclusion.

Some may have interpreted this change as another democratic scandal. To me, it was a great example of an innovative solution to an age-old problem. The other benefit of this system is that the judges weren't limited to two days a year to figure out the best work. It's an ongoing and living experience, with judges constantly ranking and discovering new artists and the crowd constantly giving feedback on what ideas are great.

Which brings us to the purpose of this chapter. A main goal of this book is to show how a balanced approach to marketing is the best solution. And when it comes to how we judge creative ideas, we should also use a balanced approach. Not all emotion similar to traditional award shows. And not all logic, like you get from a focus group. But more of a balanced solution that includes both expert peer review and input from the crowd.

We may not have the perfect answer, but the Behance solution was certainly a step in the right direction. Others will continue to innovate and move beyond traditional methods of judging creative ideas in a day, biased focus groups, or inaccurate crowd data.

Some award shows are already trying a more balanced approach. Work is sent to each judge weeks in advance so that they can review at a more comfortable pace.

But like the mission statement from Victors and Spoils, not every creative director is so smart they understand the perspective of every audience. They understand the need for experts and audiences.

We need to find ways to judge creative that employs the best practices of intuitive thinking. We need to consider both emotional and logical ways of judging. We need to allow time for our subconscious to process. We need to ensure that we are both intuitive and objective at the same time, so that all types of work are judged on equal footing. Without biases and without people gaming the system. Only then will we know the true "people's choice" for the best ideas.

Chapter 16

CREATIVITY IS THE BOTTOM LINE

In all aspects of digital and traditional marketing, art and copy are deeply connected. A picture is worth a thousand words. And a headline can be worth a thousand images. The yin and yang of copy and design are critical to creating effective communications.

Today, companies are finally understanding the essential role of creativity in business. There are plenty of case studies of famous tech companies and startups, where the design of the product created a substantial business advantage over the competition.

Through a variety of studies and reports, this chapter is included to give additional proof of the impact that creative ideas have on the bottom line.

Companies that don't make design a central role in business decisions will soon be replaced my more aggressive startups or competitors who understand the value of design.

In a research study performed by Forrester called "The Creative Dividend," they explored how creativity impacts business results. The study surveyed more than three hundred senior managers from corporations across a diverse set of industries.

The results of the study offered great insight into the normally intangible connection of creativity and business impact. A major highlight of the report stated, "Companies that embrace creativity outperform peers and competitors on key business performance indicators, including revenue growth, market share, and talent acquisition. They enjoy a high-performance working environment, driven by progressive leaders and managers who provide processes, methods, and funding to back creative initiatives."[97]

That's a bold statement. If you embrace creativity and design, you'll be more profitable. You'll beat the competition. And you'll get better employees.

More than that, the study goes on to give specific metrics of what design-led companies can expect. Companies that encourage creativity enjoy a greater market share by a factor of 1.5 to their competition. They also achieved a 10 percent or greater revenue growth than their peers by 3.5 to 1. And 82 percent of these companies believe there's a strong connection between creativity and business results.[98]

These results help underscore the need for great design and creative ideas, not just in marketing, but as a core principle of any business.

Many other studies have come to a similar conclusion, that creative ideas and great design are better for the bottom line. For example, several reports published by IPA/Gunn tested the impact of creativity on effectiveness, including their famous report, "The Link between Creativity and Effectiveness." Over a sixteen-year period, they tested hundreds of campaigns, both creative and less creative.

What they learned is that creative campaigns are up to twelve times more effective than non-creative campaigns. More than that, creative campaigns are more efficient, drive more buzz, and earn a higher share of market.[99]

The IPA/Gunn report also found that the benefit of creativity dramatically increases as the budget rises, based on the results that creative campaigns have driven twice as much market share as non-creative campaigns. They also noted the link between creative campaigns and emotional communications, with creative campaigns incorporating a higher percentage of emotion than non-creative campaigns—which led to higher rates of effectiveness.

Peter Field, the author of the report, stated, "Creativity is not the risky adventure that many in general management would appear to believe, it is becoming even safer over time. Without a doubt, it is becoming increasingly essential in ensuring a brand is successful across a wide range of business metrics from penetration to share and profit growth, and for the long term."[100]

For business leaders who feel that emotional ideas are scary, this is great news. A third-party analyst confirmed that creativity is the safe option. It doesn't need to feel risky just because we feel something. And just like the other reports, Field also showed that creative campaigns are more successful across business metrics such as an increase in sales volume, market penetration, customer acquisition, and loyalty.

In a follow-up report, Millward Brown conducted a separate test with their database (the largest pre-testing database in the world) to see if they would find similar results. They tested a wider range of creative award shows and the connection between campaigns that won and effectiveness.

What they determined is that creative ads benefit from both enjoyment and involvement, and they tend to be different from other advertising. They also tend to stimulate an emotional response. There is no single emotion that worked better than others, but any advertising that stimulates an emotional response is more effective and more memorable.[101]

They highlighted the fact that creative ideas should be encouraged, along with an appropriate strategy. (That's the balance we've been discussing.) But they also put an emphasis on a third term—branding. In order to get the best results, you should start with strategic guidance, create an experience with a creative idea, and make sure it's all connected with a strong brand.

These studies and many more were the basis of a book written by James Hurman. In *The Case for Creativity*, he combined data from fifteen independent studies on the connection between creativity and effective advertising, from research companies across the globe.

In addition to research supporting the main idea that creative ideas are more effective, he highlighted other interesting insights. For example, creative campaigns are actually more predictable than non-creative campaigns. Meaning that the results from creative campaigns are actually less risky than a straightforward message. This also goes completely against the notion that creativity is risky.[102]

Other insights include the fact that when companies have been more focused on creativity, they experience a higher growth in stock price compared to the S&P500 average.

Creative ideas are twice as likely to generate fame and media buzz, both online and offline. And campaigns with this form of fame are the most effective of all campaigns.[103]

Creative ideas promote increased and more intense attention to advertising.[104]

Creative advertising was up to nine times more likely to be recalled unprompted than advertising in general.[105]

And finally, creativity triggers greater purchase intent because it increases open mindedness and curiosity. Consumers let down their defenses more for creative ideas, allowing themselves to be sold to more readily.[106]

The future of creativity is you.

All of these studies are great resources to prove that creativity is necessary. But on their own, they aren't enough. The reality is that nothing will change unless we all become champions of creativity.

We're pushing against centuries of culture and tradition that logic is king. Today, we have plenty of arguments to make a strong case for business leaders to embrace creative ideas. Yet many still resist the idea.

In my experience, the only time this topic seems to be discussed is while reviewing a campaign or ad that's currently due. People are frustrated, and they want to approve something quickly.

But in the heat of the moment, it's hard to get past personal bias and change our perspective. Even if there aren't any studies that contradict the idea that creativity is better. People still resist.

I've found that having a discussion at a time when deadlines are not creating stress is a great way to progress. After all, the argument of this book isn't that creativity is king and logic is worthless. Instead, it's all about a balance of both. Building on a framework that you need both in business helps us find common ground.

The intersection of data-driven marketing and creative ideas is the perfect place to succeed. Together, we can end this age-old battle and bring both ideas to the table on equal footing.

We can believe in data-driven marketing and still believe in creative ideas. The two don't have to be mutually exclusive.

However, this future will only happen with a bit of work. The more we are all educated on both the data that supports creativity and having a better understanding of how emotions affect the way we think, the greater the chance that the business world will come around.

And it starts with you.

Share ideas from reports on creativity. Share a video on this topic. Have a discussion with a client or stakeholder long before the marketing campaign is created.

As creative champions, we can all help change business culture. Because today more than ever, we know that creativity is better for the bottom line.

Chapter 17

THE NEXT GOLDEN AGE OF MARKETING

Back in the '80s and '90s, advertising experienced a golden age of creativity. We didn't have a lot of data to back up our ideas. We couldn't really measure it. We just had a solid feeling in our guts.

Today we're experiencing an explosion of data. Everything is being measured. Your watch is measuring your health. Your car is calculating your attention. And your house is monitoring your purchasing habits.

We no longer have to guess. We have the data. But science doesn't have to eliminate our creativity. Rather, it can empower it.

With all that we know about emotion and decision making, we now have the data to validate our creative ideas. That's right, science is now proving that emotional ideas aren't just fluffy. They're critical to success.

Many digital marketers have already understood the significance of neuromarketing. They understand the two systems in our minds and they know how important it is to use both our conscious and subconscious in our marketing messaging. The perfect balance of strategy and creativity is the new reality.

With science finally supporting creativity, we are at the beginning of a new golden age of creativity. Creativity doesn't have to be a soft art. It can be integrated into hard data science. With this balance, marketers have an amazing opportunity to build experiences like we've never imagined.

Today's business leaders understand the importance of design-led companies. They value innovation and visionary ideas. And they have more than enough data to inspire and optimize experiences for every customer.

Business leaders know that you need *both* a great idea and a great strategy. You can optimize a mediocre idea to death and you'll get marginal results. But when you optimize a big creative idea, you experience phenomenal results.

We should no longer fight our way up the chain, afraid of pitching emotional ideas. Company executives who are up to date with the latest trends should already be transforming their companies to prioritize deeply emotional customer experiences. The companies that will thrive in the future will have already integrated design and art and data into mission critical business decisions.

This integration of creativity is no longer optional. The balance of art and science should be baked into the core of every business.

At no other time in history have we had the ability to know so much about how to connect with customers. We can fine-tune our marketing plans down to the individual. More than that, we can personalize every single step along an individual customer journey. We can serve the right mix of emotion and logic so that they like our brands and remain loyal to them.

Already we are witnessing amazing leaps in innovation. The marketplace is more level. Technology and great ideas are disrupting everything. And for those who are excited to try new ideas, there is no better time to innovate.

There's a famous quote from Bill Bernbach from back in the original golden age of creativity. He said, "We are so busy measuring public opinion that we forget we can mold it. We are so busy listening to statistics we forget we can create them."[107]

He believed that a big idea can change the world. Far too often we let the data kill creativity. Today, we can still mold public opinion. But now the right data can actually help inspire another leap in innovation. We just need to harness the power of both. And not be afraid to stand up for creativity armed with data at our side.

The world needs ideas. Ideas that are both creative and strategic. Ideas that light up the whole brain.

If there's one takeaway from this book, it's that creative ideas matter. That they really can impact the bottom line. And these big ideas are your best chance for success.

If businesses hope to improve the bottom line, they need to focus on ROI—a return on ideas.

Russell, I haven't forgotten.

More than five years have passed since I presented that billboard campaign to Russell. I'm certain he didn't think much about his question. It was just another rhetorical inquiry. I'm not sure he ever expected an answer. Or how much it would drive my focus over the following years to find one.

We continued to work together for another year. We became great friends, well beyond a client/agency relationship. We played on an indoor soccer team for many seasons. We joined a book club. We had many barbecues and attended events together. We even a took our families to Disneyland.

Since then, both of us have moved on to new jobs. I work for Adobe, a company that lives on the intersection of data and creativity. He now works for a university, guiding student entrepreneurs in building new companies.

But we never resolved that conversation. His question has been constantly on my mind as I've continued to search for an acceptable solution.

Is there any proof that creative ideas work better?

My response in this book isn't the end of the discussion. I haven't exhausted all the research. Future studies will continue to give a better answer.

But my hope is that this book at least contains the core of an answer. It offers a collection of research and science to logically prove why emotional ideas matter.

I'm excited to finally share *my* response.

No, I didn't forget Russell's question.

It just took me five years to answer.

ABOUT THE AUTHOR

For the past 23 years, Adam W Morgan has worked in the advertising and marketing industry. He has worked for many international brands from both an agency and company perspective. His creative work has won awards from the *One Show* to local *Addys*. He was named one of the 40 under 40 business leaders by *Utah Business Magazine*, and Advertising Professional of the Year for Utah in 2014 by the *American Advertising Federation*.

Currently he is a Senior Creative Director at Adobe. He ensures that the writing and creative execution is world class across the enterprise, from long-form thought leadership to Adobe.com. He has published many articles on managing creative teams and data-driven creativity, helping both creative professionals and digital marketers understand the balance of data, strategy, and creative ideas. Adam resides in Salt Lake City, Utah.

REFERENCES

Endnotes

1   David Ogilvy, *Ogilvy on Advertising* (New York: Vintage, 1985).

2   Evelyn Bernbach, *Bill Bernbach's Book: A History of Advertising that Changed the History of Advertising* (New York: Villard, 1987).

3   Bernbach, *Bill Bernbach's Book*.

4   TBWA\Chiat\Day\LA, "'Most ideas are a bit scary, and if an idea isn't scary, it's not an idea at all,'" Twitter, June 18, 2013, https://twitter.com/tbwachiatla/status/347080873327337472.

5   Jeffrey Tjendra, "The Origins of Design Thinking," *Wired*, https://www.wired.com/insights/2014/04/origins-design-thinking/.

6   CNBC. S&P Extinction. June 4, 2015.

7   Wikipedia, s.v. "Intel," last modified August 8, 2018, 05:21, https://en.wikipedia.org/wiki/Intel.

8   "Roger Wolcott Sperry ~ Life and Works," http://rogersperry.org.

9   Ziganshina, Dina, "Roger Sperry's Split Brain Experiments (1959–1968)". *Embryo Project Encyclopedia* (2017-

12-27). ISSN: 1940-5030 http://embryo.asu.edu/handle/10776/13035.

10 *Introduction to Psychology Gateways to Mind and Behavior.* ISBN 9781111833633

11 Wikipedia, s.v. "Kim Peek," last modified July 9, 2018, 15:14, https://en.wikipedia.org/wiki/Kim_Peek.

12 "Cameron's Story," The Hemispherectomy Foundation, 2008–09, http://hemifoundation.homestead.com/cameronsstory.html; "How Rasmussen's Encephalitis, a rare and deadly brain disorder, has left Cameron Mott living with half a brain," Extraordinary Children, http://mymultiplesclerosis.co.uk/ec/cameron-mott-living-half-brain/.

13 Learning Technics: Turning Teaching into Learning, www.learningtechnics.com.

14 James Randerson, "How many neurons make a human brain? Billions fewer than we thought," *The Guardian*, February 28, 2012, https://www.theguardian.com/science/blog/2012/feb/28/how-many-neurons-human-brain.

15 Randerson, "How many neurons make a human brain?"

16 Wikipedia, s.v. "Triune brain," last modified August 2, 2018, 17:31, https://en.wikipedia.org/wiki/Triune_brain.

17 Georg F. Striedter, *Principles of Brain Evolution* (New York: Oxford University Press, 2004).

18 Steve Twomey, "Phineas Gage: Neuroscience's Most Famous Patient," *Smithsonian Magazine*, Smithsonian.com, January 2010, http://www.smithsonianmag.com/history/phineas-gage-neurosciences-most-famous-patient-11390067/?no-ist.

19 Wikipedia, s.v. "Phineas Gage," last modified August 6, 2018, 10:28, https://en.wikipedia.org/wiki/Phineas_Gage.

20 Antonio R. Damasio, *Descartes' Error* (New York: G.P. Putnam's Sons, 1994).

21 Wikipedia, s.v. "René Descartes," last modified August 6, 2018, 06:13, https://en.wikipedia.org/wiki/René_Descartes.

22 Leda Cosmides and John Tooby, "Evolutionary Psychology: A Primer," University of California Santa Barbara, 1997, http://www.cep.ucsb.edu/primer.html.

23 Cosmides and Tooby, "Evolutionary Psychology."

24 Ken Robinson, *Out of Our Minds: Learning to Be Creative* (Mankato, MN: Capstone, 2011).

25 Robinson, *Out of Our Minds.*

26 Robinson, *Out of Our Minds.*

27 Daniel Pink, *A Whole New Mind: Why Right-Brainers Will Rule the World* (New York: Riverhead Books, 2006).

28 Pink, *A Whole New Mind.*

29 Shantanu Narayen, keynote speech, Adobe Summit 2016, Las Vegas, NV.

30 "2015 dmi:Design Value Index Results and Commentary," DMI:Design Management Institute, http://www.dmi.org/?page=2015DVIandOTW.

31 Richard Dickson, keynote speech, Adobe Summit, 2016, Las Vegas, NV.

32 Gary Vaynerchuk, "Every Company is a Media Company," GaryVaynerchuk.com, 2014, https://www.garyvaynerchuk.com/every-company-is-a-media-company/.

33 Vaynerchuk, "Every Company is a Media Company."

34 Vaynerchuk, "Every Company is a Media Company

35 Bob Bedore, in discussion with the author, Utah, 2016.

36 Bedore, discussion.

37 Bedore, discussion.

38 Richard H. Thaler and Cass R. Sunstein, *Nudge: Improving Decisions about Health, Wealth, and Happiness* (New Haven, CT: Yale University Press, 2008).

39 Cosmides and Tooby, "Evolutionary Psychology."

40 David Eagleman, *Incognito: The Secret Lives of the Brain* (New York: Vintage, 2012).

41 George A. Miller, "The Magical Number Seven, Plus or Minus Two: Some Limits on Our Capacity for Processing Information," *The Psychological Review* 63 (1956): 81–97.

42 Amanda L. Gilchrist, Nelson Cowan, and Moshe Naveh-Benjamin, "Working Memory Capacity for Spoken Sentences Decreases with Adult Aging: Recall of Fewer, but not Smaller Chunks in Older Adults," *Memory* 16, no. 7 (October 2008): 773–87.

43 Nelson Cowan, "The Magical Mystery Four: How Is Working Memory Capacity Limited, and Why?," *Current Directions in Psychological Science* 19, no. 1 (February 2010): 51–57.

44 "Memory Capacity of Brain is 10 Times More than Previously Thought," Salk, January 20, 2016, http://www.salk.edu/news-release/memory-capacity-of-brain-is-10-times-more-than-previously-thought/.

45 Jonah Lehrer, *How We Decide* (New York: Mariner Books, 2010).

46 Lehrer, *How We Decide*.

47 James McKeen Cattell, "The Time Taken Up by Cerebral Operations," *Mind* 11 (1887): 524–38.

48 Image from Adobe Stock

49 https://archive.org/details/NIST_9-11_Release_29

50 Douglas Fox, "Brain-Like Chip May Solve Computers' Big Problem: Energy," *Discover Magazine*, November 6, 2009, http://discovermagazine.com/2009/oct/06-brain-like-chip-may-solve-computers-big-problem-energy/.

51 Dr. Scott Steffensen, in discussion with the author, 2016.

52 Erik Du Plessis, *The Advertised Mind: Groundbreaking Insights into How Our Brains Respond to Advertising* (London: Kogan Page, 2008).

53 Du Plessis, *The Advertised Mind*.

54 Wikipedia, s.v. "Spindle neuron," last modified August 6, 2018, 14:53, https://en.wikipedia.org/wiki/Spindle_neuron.

55 Wikipedia, s.v. "Spindle neuron."

56 Ogilvy, *Ogilvy on Advertising*.

57 Wikpedia, s.v. "David Kirby (poet)," last modified March 7, 2016, 16:54, https://en.wikipedia.org/wiki/David_Kirby_(poet).

58 Wikipedia, s.v. "Jacques Prévert," last modified July 30, 2018, 17:57, https://en.wikipedia.org/wiki/Jacques_Prévert.

59 Jackie Barrie, "The story of 'the story of a sign,'" Jackie Barrie, July 9, 2014, http://jackiebarrie.com/the-story-of-the-story-of-a-sign/.

60 *Unforgettable*, directed by Eric Williams, featuring Brad Williams, Robert Bazell, and Larry Cahill (California: Rona Edwards Productions, Xeitgeist Entertainment Group, 2010), 88 min.

61 Dheeraj S. Roy et al., "Memory retrieval by activating engram cells in mouse models of early Alzheimer's disease," *Nature* 531, no. 7595 (2016): 508–12.

62 Russell A. Poldrack and Mark G. Packard, "Competition among multiple memory systems: converging evidence from animal and human brain studies," *Neuropsychologia* 41, no. 3 (2003): 245–51.

63 S. L. Rauch, L. M. Shin, and E. A. Phelps, "Neurocircuitry models of posttraumatic stress disorder and extinction: human neuroimaging research—past, present, and future," *Biological Psychiatry* 60, no. 4 (2006): 376–82.

64 Rauch, Shin, and Phelps, "Neurocirucuitry models."

65 "Memories Lost to Alzheimer's Can Be Found," *Neuroscience News*, March 16, 2016, http://neurosciencenews.com/optogenetics-alzheimers-memory-retrieval-3867/?utm_source=feedburner&utm_medium=feed&utm_campaign=Feed%3A+neuroscience-rss-feeds-neuroscience-news+%28Neuroscience+News+Updates%29.

66 Dr. Carmen Simon, "Bringing neuroscience to the world of data-driven marketing," Adobe Summit 2015, Las Vegas, NV.

67 "Adobe Named a Leader in Gartner 2017 Magic Quadrant for Digital Marketing Analytics," Adobe Newsroom, October 13, 2017, https://news.adobe.com/press-release/experience-cloud/adobe-named-leader-gartner-2017-magic-quadrant-digital-marketing.

68 Joseph A. Mikels et al., "Should I Go With My Gut? Investigating the Benefits of Emotional-Focused Decision Making," *Emotion* 11, no. 4 (2011): 743–53.

69 Mikels et al., "Should I Go With My Gut?"

70 Chip Heath and Dan Heath, *Made to Stick: Why Some Ideas Survive and Others Die* (New York: Random House, 2007).

71 Du Plessis, *The Advertised Mind.*

72 Du Plessis, *The Advertised Mind.*

73 David Edelman and Marc Singer, "The new consumer decision journey," McKinsey&Company, October 2015, http://www.mckinsey.com/business-functions/marketing-and-sales/our-insights/the-new-consumer-decision-journey.

74 Dan Greenberg, in discussion with the author, 2016.

75 Neil Patel, "The Definitive Guide to Writing a Headline that Doesn't Suck (Tips, Tactics & Tools Included)," NeilPatel.com, https://neilpatel.com/blog/write-better-headlines/.

76 Ap Dijksterhuis et al., "On Making the Right Choice: The Deliberation-Without-Attention Effect," *Science* 311, no. 5763 (2006): 1005–7.

77 Lehrer, *How We Decide.*

78 Tyler England, in discussion with the author, June 2016.

79 England, discussion.

80 England, discussion.

81 England, discussion.

82 "Strength in Numbers: Best practices in data-driven marketing," Adobe webinar, https://seminars.adobeconnect.com/_a227210/p77ute27cf2/.

83 Robert Rose and Zaan Aeck, interview, Adobe Summit 2016, Las Vegas, NV, March 2016.

84 Rose and Aeck, interview.

85 Rose and Aeck, interview.

86 Rana June, Think Tank interview, Adobe Summit 2017, Las Vegas, NV.

87 Paul J. Zak, "Why Inspiring Stories Make Us React: The Neuroscience of Narrative," *Cerebrum* (2015): 2.

88 Paul Greenberg and Robert Rose, interview, Adobe Summit 2016, Las Vegas, NV.

89 Greenberg and Rose, interview.

90 Steve Gustavson, in discussion with the author, June 2016.

91 Theodore Roosevelt, "The Man in the Arena," Excerpt from the speech "Citizenship In A Republic," delivered at the Sorbonne, in Paris, France, on April 23, 1910, Theodore-Roosevelt.com, http://www.theodore-roosevelt.com/trsorbonne-speech.html.

92 Justin M. Berg, "Balancing on the Creative High-Wire: Forecasting the Success of Novel Ideas in Organizations," *Administrative Science Quarterly* 61, no. 3 (2016): 433–68.

93 Mark Ingwer, *Empathetic Marketing* (New York: Palgrave Macmillan, 2012).

94 Victors and Spoils website, http://www.victorsandspoils.com.

95 Wikipedia, s.v. "RRS *Sir David Attenborough*," last modified July 28, 2018, 15:14, https://en.wikipedia.org/wiki/RRS_Sir_David_Attenborough; Tiffany Ap, "Landslide win for 'Boaty McBoatface' in $300M research ship naming poll," CNN, April 18, 2016, http://www.cnn.com/2016/04/18/world/boaty-mcboatface-wins-vote.

96 Scott Belsky, keynote speech, Adobe MAX 2014, Los Angeles, CA.

97 "The Creative Dividend: How Creativity Impacts Business Results," Forrester Consulting, commissioned by Adobe,

August 2014, https://landing.adobe.com/dam/downloads/whitepapers/55563.en.creative-dividends.pdf.

98 "The Creative Dividend."

99 Peter Field, "The link between creativity and effectiveness," IPA/Gunn, June 9, 2011, https://www.thinkbox.tv/Research/Thinkbox-research/The-link-between-creativity-and-effectiveness.

100 Field, "The link between creativity and effectiveness."

101 Dominic Twose and Polly Wyn Jones, "Creative Effectiveness," Admap, November 2011, http://www.millwardbrown.com/docs/default-source/insight-documents/articles-and-reports/MillwardBrown_AdMap_CreativeEffectiveness_11_2011.pdf.

102 James Hurman, The Case for Creativity (Cannes, France: Cannes Lions Publishing, 2016).

103 Field, "The link between creativity and effectiveness."

104 Rik Pieters, Luk Warlop, and Michel Wedel, "Breaking Through the Clutter: Benefits of Advertising Originality and Familiarity for Brand Attention and Memory," Management Science 48, no. 6 (2002): 765–81.

105 Brian D. Till and Daniel W. Baack, "Recall and Persuasion: Does Creative Advertising Matter?," Journal of Advertising 34, no. 3 (2005): 47–57.

106 Xiaojing Yang and Robert E. Smith, "Beyond Attention Effects: Modeling the Persuasive and Emotional Effects of Advertising Creativity," Marketing Science 28, no. 5 (2009): 809–1007.

107 Bernbach, Bill Bernbach's Book.

 Morgan James makes all of our titles available
through the Library for All Charity Organization.

www.LibraryForAll.org

Printed in the USA
CPSIA information can be obtained
at www.ICGtesting.com
JSHW022325140824
68134JS00019B/1302